The Byzantine Empire

A Captivating Guide to Byzantium and How the Eastern Roman Empire Was Ruled by Emperors such as Constantine the Great

© **Copyright 2018**

All Rights Reserved. No part of this book may be reproduced in any form without permission in writing from the author. Reviewers may quote brief passages in reviews.

Disclaimer: No part of this publication may be reproduced or transmitted in any form or by any means, mechanical or electronic, including photocopying or recording, or by any information storage and retrieval system, or transmitted by email without permission in writing from the publisher.

While all attempts have been made to verify the information provided in this publication, neither the author nor the publisher assumes any responsibility for errors, omissions or contrary interpretations of the subject matter herein.

This book is for entertainment purposes only. The views expressed are those of the author alone, and should not be taken as expert instruction or commands. The reader is responsible for his or her own actions.

Adherence to all applicable laws and regulations, including international, federal, state and local laws governing professional licensing, business practices, advertising and all other aspects of doing business in the US, Canada, UK or any other jurisdiction is the sole responsibility of the purchaser or reader.

Neither the author nor the publisher assumes any responsibility or liability whatsoever on the behalf of the purchaser or reader of these materials. Any perceived slight of any individual or organization is purely unintentional.

Free Bonus from Captivating History (Available for a Limited time)

Hi History Lovers!

Now you have a chance to join our exclusive history list so you can get your first history ebook for free as well as discounts and a potential to get more history books for free! Simply visit the link below to join.

Captivatinghistory.com/ebook

Also, make sure to follow us on:

Twitter: @Captivhistory

Facebook: Captivating History:@captivatinghistory

Contents

INTRODUCTION 1

CHAPTER 1 – LAYING THE FOUNDATION FOR THE BYZANTINE EMPIRE 4
  How Diocletian Changed Rome Forever 4
  The Rise of Constantine 6

CHAPTER 2 – THE AGE OF CONSTANTINE 9
  Conquering the East 10
  A Fresh Start: The New Capital of the Roman Empire 12
  The Last Years of Constantine the Great: A Dark Secret, Baptism, and Death 13

CHAPTER 3 – FROM CONSTANTINE'S DEATH TO THE FALL OF THE WESTERN EMPIRE 15
  Julian the Apostate: Zeus Strikes Back 16
  Further Decay: Valentinian, Valens, and Gratian 19
  Theodosius to the Rescue 20
  The Sack of Rome 21
  The Huns 21
  The Final Fall of the Western Empire and the Resilience of the East .. 22

CHAPTER 4 – THE AGE OF JUSTINIAN, THE GREATEST RULER OF THE BYZANTINE EMPIRE 25
  The Coronation of Justinian and Theodora 26
  The Roman Law 28
  Belisarius, the Superior General 28
  The Nika Revolt 29
  The Byzantine Golden Age 30
  Belisarius Retakes the Provinces 31
  The Hard Times: the Plague 31

CHAPTER 5 – HERACLIUS 34
  The War against the Persians 35
  Cultural Changes 36
  The Muslim Attack 36

CHAPTER 6 – THE ICONOCLASTS: LEO III THE ISAURIAN AND CONSTANTINE V 38

- THE BYZANTINE ICONOCLASM 39
- CONSTANTINE V 41

CHAPTER 7 – THE COLDBLOODED EMPRESS IRENE OF ATHENS ... 42
- THE END OF ICONOCLASM 43
- MOTHER AND SON 43
- MEANWHILE IN ROME 44

CHAPTER 8 – TINY STEPS FORWARD: THEOPHILUS AND MICHAEL THE DRUNKARD 46
- THE CULTURAL RENAISSANCE UNDER THEOPHILUS 46
- NEW CHRISTIANS 47
- MILITARY RECOVERY UNDER MICHAEL THE DRUNKARD (AND HIS UNCLE) 48

CHAPTER 9 – A NEW GOLDEN AGE: BASIL THE MACEDONIAN AND HIS DYNASTY 49
- THE DRUNKARD'S SON, LEO VI THE WISE 50
- THE LOVE LIFE OF AN EMPEROR: LEO AND TWO ZOES 51
- ALL THE REGENT RULERS OF YOUNG EMPEROR CONSTANTINE VII 52
- CONSTANTINE VII "THE PURPLE-BORN" 54
- ROMANUS II AND THEOPHANO 56

CHAPTER 10 – THE CHANGE IN THE HOUSE OF MACEDON: NICEPHORUS PHOCAS AND HIS NEPHEW 58
- THE EMPEROR NICEPHORUS AND THEOPHANO 59
- IMPERIAL EXPANSION UNDER NICEPHORUS 59
- THE HOLY MOUNTAIN 60
- DECLINE AND DEATH 61
- THE EMPEROR JOHN I TZIMISCES 61

CHAPTER 11 – BASIL II THE BULGAR SLAYER 63
- THE RISE OF THE LEGITIMATE EMPEROR 64
- ALLIANCE WITH THE RUSSIANS 64
- THE BULGAR SLAYER 65

CHAPTER 12 – ALEXIUS COMNENUS 66
- A FAULTY START 67
- ALTERNATIVE WAYS 67
- THE FIRST CRUSADE 68
- MANUEL I COMNENUS 70

CHAPTER 13 – THE COLLAPSE AND FALL OF THE EASTERN ROMAN EMPIRE 71
- THE FATAL CRUSADE 72

THE AFTERMATH OF DESTRUCTION AND A SHORT-LIVED RECOVERY 72
MICHAEL PALAEOLOGUS 73
THE OTTOMANS 74
THE LAST EMPEROR OF CONSTANTINOPLE 76

CONCLUSION 78

THE TIMELINE OF THE BYZANTINE EMPERORS 79

READ MORE CAPTIVATING HISTORY BOOKS ABOUT ANCIENT HISTORY 85

REFERENCES 88

Introduction

Long after the Western Roman Empire ceased to exist, another Roman Empire was alive and well. This empire was the only organized state in the Western world which persisted in the same shape from antiquity until the dawn of the modern age. Unaffected by the Dark Ages, this society was a fusion of ancient Greece, Rome, and Christianity – a fusion that grew and matured centuries before the Renaissance.

The Byzantine Empire was founded during the chaotic third century. It was the time when revolts and civil wars were common, and Roman emperors merely lasted for a year. In the midst of this turmoil, the new hierarchical, ordered world arose on the Bosphorus River. But the Eastern Roman Empire wasn't a typical autocratic society. Anyone, including humble farmers and orphaned women, had a chance to find their way onto the throne. Byzantium's greatest ruler was formerly a lowly peasant from present-day Macedonia, while one empress was an ex-courtesan.

Despite being a deeply religious society, its educational system was thorough and surprisingly secular. There were no Dark Ages in Byzantium. This part of the world was the guardian of light and civilization in Medieval Europe and beyond.[i] It presented a shield that protected the rest of Europe from rapidly expanding Islamic forces.[ii] At the same time, it preserved invaluable texts and artifacts of the

Greek and Latin culture – and created more. The mosaics of Ravenna were the work of Byzantine artisans, as was the Hagia Sofia. The timeless Roman law, which served as a basis and inspiration for a great majority of European legal systems was created in Constantinople, not Rome. It wasn't introduced by Octavian, Claudius, or Trajan. The name of the mighty emperor who gave us such achievement was Justinian.

Byzantine Empire was not the real name of this state. It was formally known as the Eastern Roman Empire. The citizens of Constantinople and its rulers saw themselves as Romans, not Byzantine. Not just them – their neighboring countries including their enemies saw this empire as Roman. When Constantinople fell after eleven centuries, the Ottoman sultan Mehmed II took the title Caesar of Rome. It wasn't until eighteenth century that the scholars of the west denied the Eastern Empire the tag "Roman." Byzantium – the name of a tiny town which served as a basis of Constantinople – has become the official name of this state centuries after it collapsed.

The Eastern and Western world were loosely linked by Christianity until 1054 when the church split into Catholic and Orthodox halves. The hostility culminated during the Crusades. The Eastern Empire never fully recovered from the violent assaults from the Catholic West. It lost the capacity to resist the Ottomans' invasion. When it fell, it was quickly forgotten. Out of sheer ignorance, its new name, Byzantine, became the synonym for obscurity and even deviousness.

The history of the Byzantine Empire is a lesser known one, yet it is among the most captivating. This book is a story of power and glory, anarchy and order, paganism and Christianity, war and peace, the West and the East. You'll get familiar with the roots of the greatest controversies that defined the history of Europe and the entirety of Western civilization – the conflict between the Catholic and Orthodox churches, and the one between Christianity and Islam. You'll read the stories of remarkable emperors you've never heard of and about the astonishing bravery of Graeco-Roman heroes such as Constantine Dragases, who resisted the Ottomans until the end, and Belisarius, who fought the Persians to reconquer what used to be the Western Empire.

The story of Constantinople began in 324 AD when Constantine decided – or was told by a divine voice, as the ancient legend says – to establish the new capital of the world on a hill upon the Bosphorus. Europe was still Roman, but the city of Rome was not as important. It belonged to the past, just like the ancient city of Troy. Byzantium was the future – a very promising and dynamic one, as we will see in the following pages.

The Western Empire continued to exist in some form for another century and a half after Constantinople was built. The two empires lived simultaneously, and a few rulers managed to reunite them occasionally, but only for a brief couple of years or so until one day, the barbaric King Odoacer took the West and sent the Western imperial regalia to the Eastern emperor.

Our story begins with the period called Late Roman Empire, which started with Diocletian and was profoundly influenced by Constantine the Great. The first three chapters cover the struggle of the two halves of the Roman world, the ways their emperors tried to resist enemies outside and within the borders until the final fall of Rome. The rest of the book addresses the Roman "future," the new world that was just as mighty as Augustan Rome, and the most glorious (and equally controversial) figures of the "New Rome" – the Byzantine Emperor Justinian and Empress Theodora.

Chapter 1 – Laying the Foundation for the Byzantine Empire

Constantine's vision and energy were remarkable, but the founding of the new Roman capital would be impossible if it weren't for Diocletian and his profound reforms. He brought changes that affected almost every aspect of Roman society. Some of them were popular, others were not, but he certainly knew what he was doing.

The third century was a time of tremendous suffering for the Roman people. The days of stability and glory were over. Armies fought each other within the Empire, while barbarian hordes attacked the frontiers. The populace was drowning in debt and ever-increasing taxes. Twenty-nine emperors tried to establish new dynasties. All of them ended up murdered, more often by the Praetorian Guard than by outside forces – all but one.

How Diocletian Changed Rome Forever

Diocletian was a soldier from Dalmatia (in present-day Croatia). He gained power in the same way as the others: by killing his predecessor and defeating his army. But he did everything else differently. He knew that the Roman Empire was too vast and complex to be controlled by a single man. Unblinded by power, he decided to share it. He made Maximian, his old drinking buddy, a co-emperor and divided the empire in half.[iii] Diocletian took control over the eastern (richer, more-cultured, and mainly Greek) half of the empire and gave his friend the western, Latin part. It all worked so well that Diocletian decided to divide the empire even further, appoint two junior emperors and establishing the tetrarchy. Officially, there was still one, unique Roman Empire. The four men had the power to lead armies and issue laws. The system was efficient, at least temporarily. Borders and provinces were under control, and Diocletian turned to other issues. He reformed the administration and made the tax system more efficient. Finally, he rebranded the institution of the Emperor of Rome. Hiding behind the symbols of the obsolete republic, which worked so well for Octavian Augustus and his descendants, was no longer appropriate. The days of the principate were over.[iv] The emperor was no longer the "first among equals." Diocletian elevated himself from the masses and was thereafter presented as the embodiment of Jupiter on Earth. Unlike the emperors from the previous epochs who used to be depicted either in togas or military uniforms, Diocletian was dressed in a golden robe and wore a crown. It was the beginning of the Dominate, or the late Roman Empire.[v]

Romans had deified their deceased emperors for centuries. As most of the populace were pagans, they easily accepted the idea of another divine ruler. But not all of them were pagans. People all throughout the empire had embraced a new religion that gave them hope against arbitrary injustice. Christianity gave them faith in an all-powerful, yet loving God who would punish the wicked and reward the just with eternal life. And the growing number of Christians in the empire weren't willing to swallow Diocletian's claims of divinity.

Christians were model citizens. They paid their taxes without complaining and were willing to serve in the army. But there was something that Diocletian couldn't tolerate. Christians undermined the essence of his imperial authority by refusing to make a sacrifice to the emperor. They insisted that there was only one God and highlighted the fact that the emperor, no matter how powerful, was just a man.

So Diocletian decided to wipe them out. Numerous churches were destroyed, and holy writings were burned. People were captured, some of them even killed, but Christianity persisted. All that repression just made it stronger. The pagans sympathized with their Christian neighbors, rejecting Diocletian's propaganda, which depicted them as immoral, godless, dangerous dissidents, and even cannibals. In reality, Christians were common people who paid taxes, had stable families, and were honest in trade. Everyone knew that. Diocletian's battle against Christianity turned against him. Finally, in 305 AD, Diocletian abdicated. Maximian, who ruled the West, had to abdicate too. Their junior emperors (Caesars), Galerius and Constantinus the Pale, had now become emperors and were requested to name their own respective Caesars. Everything went smoothly, except for one thing. Some of the tetrarchs (tetrarchy was the rule of four) had sons. Those sons weren't the least bit happy when they found out that some other men were made heirs to their fathers. The perfect order that Diocletian established had already started to melt.

The sons of Maximian and Constantinus the Pale, Maxentius, and Constantine, believed they were to become the heirs to the throne. When they discovered they were left with nothing, like ordinary private citizens, they felt betrayed. And of course, they did not accept it.

The Rise of Constantine

Unlike other tetrarchs, Constantinus the Pale was honest and down-to-earth. He never persecuted Christians or anyone else. His army – even the highest ranks – included people of all religions. Naturally, he was extremely popular with the army. But unfortunately, he was seriously ill. He wasn't 'pale' metaphorically; he was dying of leukemia. This had become clear during his campaign in Britain in early 306. He succumbed to his illness on July 25, 306. The army was informed that his junior emperor named Severus – whom most of them had never heard of – would take Constantinus' place.

Constantine often joined his father in campaigns and was there when he died. The army was loyal to him just as it was to Constantinus. So, they declared Constantine their emperor, and another civil war had begun.

Meanwhile, encouraged by the way Constantine claimed power, Maximian's son, Maxentius, seized Rome. Now there were six men claiming to be the emperors of Rome – the four 'legal' (following the system of succession established by Diocletian) tetrarchs, and two 'illegal' ones (who seized power by force) – Constantine and Maxentius. By 312, only the two intruders were left in the West. Then Constantine, with his forty thousand men, invaded Maxentius' Italy.

Unlike Constantine, Maxentius was a cruel and largely unpopular ruler. He wasn't assured that his army would defend him from Constantine, so he escaped the city. The two armies soon met at the Milvian Bridge. Constantine, who later claimed he was guided by Christ, crushed Maxentius' forces. The next day, Constantine triumphantly entered Rome holding Maxentius' head on a spear. He had become the sole ruler of the Western Roman Empire. But back in the fourth century, the West was not the best. It was just the beginning for Constantine.

The bust of Constantine the Great[vi]

Chapter 2 – The Age of Constantine

Constantine marched into Rome as a liberator who set his people free from the ruthless tyrant. The Senate hailed him enthusiastically when he entered the Forum. But then he did something unthinkable, something that no Roman Emperor had ever done in history – he refused to offer the customary sacrifice to the ancient deity of victory. He had won his victory against Maxentius wielding the cross and the sword, and with the help of the Christian God. This was a turning point in Roman history and the one that linked the Roman Empire and the Christian church forever.

His impact on Christianity was enormous, but Constantine had still not become a genuine Christian.[vii] He never renounced his title of Pontifex Maximus, and the depictions of his favorite pagan deities, Sol Invictus and Mars Conservator, still appeared on his coins. It is questionable whether he even understood the deeper meaning of Christianity and the theological concept of resurrection. Nevertheless, he was wise enough to realize that Christianity did not have to be seen as a threat to the establishment. He saw the new religion as an opportunity to prove himself as a just ruler and to unite the people within the Empire. So, he stopped all persecutions of Christians, and in 313 legalized the faith by issuing an edict of toleration. From that point on, Christianity took another purpose: to support Constantine's regime the way paganism supported Diocletian's. But he made sure not to alienate the pagans, who still made up the majority of the populace, and he still had not made the new religion the exclusive one of the empire.

Conquering the East

While Constantine was portraying himself as a model of religious toleration in the West, the East had fallen into the hands of Emperor Licinus. Licinus had gotten rid of the competition in his half of the empire, but he was afraid of Constantine. Assured that the Christians would support his western rival, he started persecuting them the way Diocletian did. Constantine saw his opportunity and came with his army. After a couple of weeks, the armies of the two Roman emperors met near the ancient Greek colony of Byzantium – which was to become the center of the known universe – where on September 18, 324, Constantine's forces completely devastated Licinus'. Constantine the Greatest, as he named himself after his triumph over Maximinus, had now become Constantine the Victor, the sole emperor of the Roman Empire.

Once again, Constantine emerged as the protector of the people. He came and saved the Christians without persecuting the pagan populace. He was carefully maintaining the guise of tolerance and neutrality until he managed to eliminate the last of his rivals. Now that he had become the sole ruler, he could embrace Christianity more openly. His mother, Helena – the world's first pilgrim – went to the Holy Land and founded numerous hostels and hospitals along the way, including the Church of the Nativity in Bethlehem, and the Church of the Holy Sepulchre at Golgotha in Jerusalem at the exact spot where Christ had been crucified, and where Hadrian later built the temple of Venus – which apparently had to be demolished.

The Church of the Holy Sepulchre, also called the Basilica of the Holy Sepulchre, or the Church of the Resurrection[viii]

This was a time of rapid change within the empire, which left far-reaching consequences. Constantine carried out a number of reforms to stabilize the shaken empire. Markets and commerce recovered, and the working classes started working again (instead of fighting in civil wars). The peasant farmers were obliged to stay on their land. The members of guilds, as well of their children, had to stay in their occupations. These changes eventually resulted in the feudal system that was common throughout the West. In the stable and prosperous East, however, these reforms had little effect.[ix]

As the material well-being improved throughout the empire, Constantine went further in nurturing Christianity. He banned pagan sacrifices and ritual orgies, put an end to the practice of crucifixion and the violent gladiatorial games (chariot races persisted as less violent), and confiscated temple treasuries to build churches.

The united Roman Empire and Christianity were linked for good, but then a new challenge arose. A young priest (and brilliant speaker) from Egypt called Arius started teaching that Christ was just not truly a god and that he was inferior to God the Father. This heresy threatened to tear the still decentralized and disorganized church apart. So, Constantine decided to put an end to the chaos and, when his idea of 'working the differences out and living in harmony' failed, he announced a great council. On May 20, 325, in Nicaea, Constantine gathered all bishops in the empire and proposed a simple solution to the complex theological issue of the nature of Christ. The Arians did not dare to disagree with the emperor, and Arius himself was condemned afterward. Constantine restored Christian unity just as he had done with the empire.

A Fresh Start: The New Capital of the Roman Empire

Now that Constantine had set everything up, he made a massive basilica in Rome, with a huge statue of himself inside, and several other churches, including one for the pope. But he preferred to live in another city and create a fresh start for the profoundly changed empire. A divine voice, as he later claimed, showed him the site where he should build New Rome (Nova Roma).

The thousand years old Greek colony called Byzantium was placed on a perfect spot between the eastern and western borders of the empire. Surrounded on three sides with water, it had incredible natural defenses. The city possessed a large harbor at the center of the lucrative trade routes between the Mediterranean and the Black Sea. Last but not least, this was the site where Constantine crushed Licinus and became the empire's sole ruler.

New Rome was built remarkably quickly in just six years. People from all parts of the empire were happy to move there and enjoy the numerous benefits, including free grain and fresh water, as well as prospects of advancement on the social ladder. The new capital was dedicated on May 11, 330, and was thereafter known as Constantinople.

The Last Years of Constantine the Great: A Dark Secret, Baptism, and Death

In his later years, Constantine struggled to preserve the political and religious harmony. He ruled oppressively and utilized severe measures to return some prosperity. He was successful in doing so, but he was also becoming increasingly ruthless. He couldn't tolerate any prospective rival and he had already killed many, but this time it was different. There was a man whom the masses loved so much and whom they wanted to see as the next emperor. This man was named Crispus, Constantine's oldest son. The emperor couldn't stand his son's popularity. He accused Crispus of attempting to seduce his stepmother, Fausta, and had both of them killed.

Despite his firm hand, Constantine couldn't control everything. He wasn't able to manage the church the way he wanted. He influenced the official doctrine established in Nicaea, but the minds and faith of ordinary people were beyond his power. Heretics such as Arius gained the support of many, even though they'd previously been banished from the church. Constantine was never sure which faction within the church was right and was always interested in supporting the one that was stronger and more popular. In the end, he was baptized by the Arian bishop called Eusebius. Trying to fortify his position, Constantine was again after military glory. In 337, he went to attack the Persians, but couldn't make it. He was too sick to fight this battle. Aware that he was dying, he needed the last-minute blessing. The emperor who had such a great impact on history by embracing

Christianity was baptized just before his death.[x] He was buried as an "equal of the apostles" in the lavish Church of the Holy Apostles in Constantinople.

Chapter 3 – From Constantine's Death to the Fall of the Western Empire

Even though the empire had been deeply transformed during the reigns of Domitian and Constantine, the citizens of both the West and East continued to identify themselves as Romans. Some of them were Christians, but paganism persisted too. The temples of the old state religion were full, as were the churches. Christianity was legal, but it still hadn't become the official faith of the empire. But that was not the only issue that Constantine left unsolved.

The late emperor didn't care who would succeed him as long as (as we've seen in the previous chapter) no one tried to replace him while he was still alive. Now that he died, his three sons – Constantine II, Constantius II, and Constans – divided the empire among themselves, but soon after, they started killing each other in order to take the whole. At the same time, Constantius II, who was the most capable of the brothers, managed to get rid of anyone who might claim to have a drop of his father's blood, with the exception of a younger cousin called Julian, who didn't seem to be much of a threat. Then, after three years, Constantius II invaded the area controlled by his youngest brother, and another period of civil war had begun.

Julian the Apostate: Zeus Strikes Back

The little Julian (Flavius Claudius Julianus, later known as Julian the Apostate), who was only five years old when his older cousins were busy fighting each other, spent his early years under a kind of house arrest. Even when he grew up, he displayed no imperial ambitions. Julian used to read the Greek and Roman classics as a child, and when he turned nineteen, he managed to get permission to travel and pursue his studies of the classical world. He traveled from Pergamum to Ephesus, learned philosophy, secretly rejected Christianity, and embraced Neoplatonism – a school of thought based on Plotinus' interpretation of Platonic philosophy. Julian was careful to keep his apostasy hidden, and he appeared to his Christian teachers as the most pious of men. But the day had come when he no longer could proceed with his life of a scholar. The emperor needed him.

Meanwhile, Constantius II managed to get rid of his brothers and take the whole empire. But Rome had so many enemies, and it was too challenging for a single ruler to manage everything. Barbarians were invading northern territories, but he needed to fight against Persia. Ironically, now all his brothers had been killed, he desperately needed someone of his blood to take care of other fronts. So, he called for Julian, gave him the rank of Caesar (junior emperor), gave him 360 utterly incapable men (who "knew only how to pray"[xi]), and sent him to Gaul.

Julian was an introverted scholar, and he had zero military experience. No one really expected he would achieve anything, but they were wrong. During the five years he spent in Gaul, he managed to organize the local army, expel the barbarians, set twenty thousand prisoners free, brought peace to the province, defeated the Germanic tribes in their own territory, took his king as the prisoner of war, and sent him to Constantinople in chains.

Constantius felt threatened by his young cousin's victory and instantly demanded money and troops from Gaul to be sent to him as a support against the Persians. Julian's men did not want to leave their families and go to the east, so they mutinied. The soldiers gathered overnight, surrounded Julian's palace, hailed him as Augustus, and demanded him to lead them against Constantius. Having received a sign from Zeus (as he claimed), Julian accepted, and another war nearly began. Since he no longer needed to pretend he was Christian, Julian sent manifestos to all important cities in order to restore Roman traditional religion. But then the news spread that Constantius died of an illness. Julian arrived in Constantinople, where he was welcomed enthusiastically by the crowds as well as the Senate.

But Julian wasn't happy. He saw decay, greed, and a lack of discipline everywhere. The empire was sick, and he blamed Christianity – with its 'feminine' attributes of kindness and forgiveness that replaced the traditional Roman sense of honor and duty – as the major cause of this decay.

Julian was smart enough to realize that persecution wouldn't work, so he published an edict of toleration. But at the same time, he proclaimed traditional Roman paganism as a superior religion. He reopened temples throughout the empire and tried several subtle measures – and some less subtle ones – to persuade the populace to return to the old religion, but without success. Then he came to the idea to enforce his ideas by a great military victory, just as Constantine had done by winning the battle of the Milvian Bridge.

Julian the Apostate[xii]

Determined to destroy Christianity, Julian sent messengers to ask the oracle at Delphi for a prophecy. The answer was not what he hoped for. The words of the oracle were: "Tell the emperor that my hall has fallen to the ground. Phoibos no longer has his house, nor his mantic bay, nor his prophetic spring; the water has dried up."[xiii]

We'll never know for sure whether this prophecy was authentic, or if it was all made up by contemporary Christians, but it wasn't the only sign that things would not end up well for Julian. He ordered the rebuilding of the ancient Jewish temple in Jerusalem just to prove that Christ was wrong when he prophesied that the temple wouldn't be restored until the end times. But the works were interrupted twice – once by an earthquake and the second time by the fire that burned the entire structure to the ground. As if this wasn't enough, the emperor was becoming increasingly unpopular day after day, especially after he closed a Christian cathedral and used the gold to pay his army. Nevertheless, he wasn't willing to give up.

In the spring of 363, he marched east to attack Persia. His army was a proper Roman army, huge and powerful, and it easily entered the Persian territory. But the Persian capital of Ctesiphon was surrounded by high walls. They couldn't break in, but they also couldn't stay around. The heat was unbearable for the Romans, and the news emerged that a large Persian army was coming, so Julian reluctantly abandoned the siege. A few months later, the Persians attacked, and Julian instantly got a fatal wound. Julian was the last pagan Roman Emperor and the attempts to restore the ancient world ended with him. He was also the last emperor from the Constantinian dynasty, and now the path was open for a new line.

Further Decay: Valentinian, Valens, and Gratian

The world continued to change, and the Roman Empire was soon flooded by Germanic tribes who came not as invaders, but as settlers who wanted to take refuge from the Huns – the new force that frightened even them. Nevertheless, they weren't willing to assimilate and accept the Roman culture, and the social patterns changed. At the same time, the empire was ruled by one incompetent emperor after another.[xiv] The first that came after Julian managed to suffocate himself by leaving a brazier burning in his tent overnight. His successors, Valentinian and Valens, divided the empire again. Valentinian ruled the West for eleven years before he died, leaving a son named Gratian as his heir. Gratian was too young and he fell under the influence of his uncle.

Valens made a deal with the two hundred thousand Visigoths and Ostrogoths who wanted to settle in the Roman territory. The newcomers would be given land in Thrace, and they would provide troops. But it did not end well. Great tensions between the locals and the newcomers escalated and, in 378, Valens and Gratian jointly (but without an accurate report or a proper plan) attacked the Goths near Adrianople. The Romans were exhausted from the long march and tortured by heat, and the Goths slaughtered two-thirds of them. This was a catastrophe that allowed every barbaric tribe to enter the empire and do whatever they pleased – and so they did. The Goths even spread east and threatened Constantinople. The situation was almost impossible to handle.

Theodosius to the Rescue

Now that Valens was dead, the western emperor, Gratian, appointed his best general, Theodosius, as the emperor of the eastern half of the empire. Tens of thousands of experienced soldiers had been killed at the Adrianople disaster, and Theodosius had to find some fresh blood quickly. He pressed virtually everyone into service, and finally let the barbarian troops in. He basically confirmed the arrangement made by Valens, but he did it smarter, paying more attention to the details. It worked at the moment, although it left disastrous consequences that would become visible within a generation: the fall of Rome and the beginning of the Dark Ages on the Western Roman Empire.

In 382, on his way to Thessalonica, Theodosius fell ill and looked as though he would die. Like Constantine, he wanted to wash his hands and be baptized before the end of his life. However, after the baptism, he recovered. This brought a deep change to the way he ruled the empire. He no longer could kill innocents or ignore the issues within the church. He dealt with the Arian heresy and, soon after, with paganism within the empire. Prompted by his religious mentor, Bishop Ambrose of Milan, Theodosius finally closed the public temples and renounced the title of Pontifex Maximus – the chief priest of the traditional Roman religion – previously held by all Roman Emperors since Augustus. He wasn't really willing to do so but was forced to. After killing a few thousand civilians to suppress a mutiny in Thessalonica, Ambrose did not allow Theodosius to enter the

Church until he made atonement. It took him months, but eventually, Theodosius apologized and performed penance.

Quickly after, he put an end to all things pagan, from the Olympic Games, to the Delphic Oracle and the Temple of Vesta. The vestal virgins were dismissed, and the eternal fire extinguished. In 391, Theodosius officially made Christianity – which had also evolved and accepted some Roman features by this point – the only religion in the empire.

The Sack of Rome

Theodosius' successors weren't strong enough to deal with the 'barbaric' elements in the empire, and Germanic and other tribes achieved enormous power. The people who controlled armies had more influence than the emperors of the East and the West. Rome was under the command of a general of Vandal origin called Stilicho, even though there was an emperor (Honorius), too. It was actually rather convenient, because Stilicho was a brilliant commander, able to put down revolts and invasions of Germanic barbarians. But, unfortunately, neither the Senate in Rome, nor the public officials in Constantinople supported him. When he tried to bribe the Visigothic King Alaric instead of fighting him (which was a reasonable decision that could save many Roman lives and postpone a catastrophe), the Emperor Honorius was persuaded that Stilicho had betrayed Rome. The mighty general was killed, and Italy was defenseless. So, in 401, Alaric's army invaded Italy. The Goths climbed the Seven Hills of Rome and ruined the city. Honorius escaped to Ravena, and the citizens of both Rome and the western provinces, such as Britania, were left to fend for themselves.

The Huns

Constantinople was still safe. The Eastern Empire kept the universal and divine entitlements of the empire. As for the West, it was doomed.

Alarmed by the sack of Rome, the new Eastern Emperor, Theodosius II, ordered massive walls constructed around Constantinople. Alaric died soon after and did not pose a threat anymore, but those walls served the Eastern Emperors well for another thousand years. In fact, they immediately proved very useful. Meanwhile, a new horrifying threat came from Asia – Attila and the Huns. The Huns gave a new meaning to the word "uncivilized." They slept on their horses, never changed clothes, never bathed or cooked their food. They were so terrifying that people throughout the empire called Attila "The Scourge of God."

Constantinople was forced to let the Huns enter the Roman territory and to give Attila enormous riches to leave them alone. But a few months later they came back because of curious circumstances. The emperor's sister, Honoria, tried her best to escape a forced marriage with a senator. When all her previous attempts failed, she sent a letter and a ring to Attila, who then came to take what was his.

There was no one left in Rome to resist Attila or try to persuade him to spare the city – except for Pope Leo. The two men met and talked, and the Huns left the city. The next morning, Attila was found dead in his tent.

The Final Fall of the Western Empire and the Resilience of the East

Attila died, and the Huns no longer threatened the Roman Empire, but the true enemy was still there, and it was not only integrated into the society, but effectively controlled it. The barbarians were just behind the throne, exercising power and controlling the emperors. When Emperor Valentinian III decided to get rid of his barbarian master, he was killed too. His widow asked the Vandals to come and help Romans. They came, sacked Rome, and took the empress with themselves to Carthage.

At the same time, Constantinople was under control of the Sarmatian General, Aspar, and his puppet-emperor, named Leo. But Leo wasn't happy with his status and was seeking the way to overthrow his master – but not the way Valentinian did in the West. Instead, he found a way to take the military control from him. With the help of the Isaurian General, Tarasicodissa, he managed to charge Aspar with treason. In turn, Tarasicodissa – now Hellenized and renamed Zeno – was given the hand of Leo's daughter and the power needed to resist Aspar.

Meanwhile, Leo decided to subjugate the Vandal kingdom of North Africa, and he used all available resources to equip the army. However, the commander in charge was the worst possible choice – his brother-in-law, called Basiliscus, who landed away from Carthage, accidentally wrecked the fleet, destroyed the army, panicked, and ran away.

Leo was succeeded by Zeno in 474, but Basiliscus and his sister, Verina, soon overthrew him, and the disgraceful commander took over the throne. He soon proved that his ability to rule was on par with his ability to lead an army. His actions provoked massive rebellion. Then Zeno returned with an army. Basiliscus' generals gladly switched sides, and so did the Senate.

While Zeno was busy reestablishing stability in the Eastern Roman Empire, the West was collapsing. In 476, a barbarian general, Odoacer, sent the teenage Emperor Romulus Augustulus into exile. Odoacer then took the crown and scepter and sent them to Zeno. The Eastern Emperor wasn't willing to support the barbaric general in taking the West, but he couldn't fight him either. Eventually, he came up with a great plan; he gave the Ostrogothic King Theodoric (who at the time was making a mess in the Balkans) authority to rule the West. The Goths overwhelmed Odoacer and settled in Italy. At the same time, the Eastern Empire finally became free from any internal barbaric influence. Zeno managed to restore stability but didn't manage to live long enough to see the new era that started thanks to his effort.

Chapter 4 – The Age of Justinian, the Greatest Ruler of the Byzantine Empire

Zeno's immediate successor was Anastasius I, who established some new, sustainable patterns of government, bureaucracy, and economic development in the Eastern Empire, reformed the taxation system, introduced a new currency, minimized corruption, and left a considerable budget surplus. He died childless and, in 518, an unlikely heir came to the throne. Justin came from a peasant family from Thrace, joined the army in Constantinople, and rose to the position of commander of the palace guard. Now, with the support of the military (encouraged by donations in silver), he became the emperor. Justin was 70 at the time and wasn't properly educated to run a state, but his nephew and adopted son, Peter Sabbatius, was both fairly young (36) and well educated. Peter was grateful for all the support he received from his uncle, which included the finest education available, and he changed his name to Justinian.

Aware of his power as the emperor's adopted son, Justinian was enthusiastic about adopting a more aggressive foreign policy. His two major goals were to retake the West and liberate Rome from the barbarians and to restore the relations with papacy and reunite the church. The news disturbed the Gothic king in Italy, who knew his rule was crumbling. However, Justinian wasn't in a hurry. He spent many days watching the chariot races at the Hippodrome, where he, unlike the rulers before him, openly supported "the Blues" against "the Greens." His hobby allowed him to connect with the vast network of citizens supporting the same team, and so he knew better than anyone else what was going on in the city on all levels. Those people gave him much valuable information, and more: they introduced him to a beautiful young actress (the word "actress" was a synonym for "prostitute" back then) named Theodora. He fell madly in love with her and, despite her status of "a lady of the stage," married her with the consent of his benevolent uncle emperor.

Justin was still the emperor, but it was Justinian who made all decisions. He offered support to the neighboring peoples that struggled under the tyrannies of their masters. The emissaries from around the region gathered in Constantinople. The city virtually became the center of the world. The vassal kings loyal to the king of Persia quickly changed sides, encouraged by the support from Constantinople. Moreover, a Byzantine army led by Justinian's bodyguard called Belisarius invaded Persian Armenia. This was just the first in the line of expansionistic actions that were soon to take place.

The Coronation of Justinian and Theodora

In 527, now seriously ill, Justin, prompted by the Senate, crowned Justinian as co-emperor. By the end of the year, Justin was dead and the empire belonged to Justinian and Theodora. They were so much different from anyone who had ever been on the throne of the Roman Empire. The coronation in Hagia Sofia was luxurious, and it anticipated a new age of glory.

Justinian believed the Roman Empire was not complete without Rome. There was one God in heaven, and there should also be only one empire on earth. Since he was the emperor, it was his responsibility to restore the heavenly order and bring those western territories back.

Justinian I the Great[xv]

The Roman Law

Although admired for his imperial goals and actions, Justinian wasn't really popular. His politics included costly military actions and construction projects, and it all came from taxes. Even the rich and privileged could not continue to escape their commitments, which increased the hostility between the nobility and the emperor. Justinian favored pragmatic individuals over blue-blooded ones and surrounded himself with a few extremely capable men. One of them was Tribonian, an amazing lawyer who knew Roman laws and edicts more than anyone else in the empire.

At the time, Roman law was a mess. Even though everything was simple at the dawn of civilization, things had seriously changed over the last thousand years, which brought numerous contradictory precedents, conflicting interpretations, and special exemptions. None of them were written down in any one place. So, Julian decided to systematize the Roman Law, remove repetitions and inconsistencies, and create a comprehensive legal code – the first one in imperial history. Tribonian made it happen; he produced the codex that was to become the basis of most legal system that we still use today.[xvi]

Belisarius, the Superior General

In 528, the Persians attacked again, this time with a large, intimidating army. The Byzantine forces led by General Belisarius not only defeated them, but also took part of Armenia. War had finally broken out with Persia, and he had been busy reorganizing the eastern army. The aging Persian king sent a huge army to flatten the Romans, but Belisarius defeated it with his characteristic flair, and he even managed to conquer part of Persian Armenia. Almost at the same time, the Vandals in North Africa overthrew their king, who was at least formally a loyal vassal to Constantinople, and sent some offensive threats. Shortly after that, Belisarius was free to deal with them too. But something unexpected was happening in Constantinople.

The Nika Revolt

While Justinian was contemplating reconquering the Roman territories, Constantinople was at the edge of revolt. High taxes and corrupt officials made the mobs angry, but there was the drop that spilled the glass. The Blues and the Greens occasionally caused incidents – pretty much like today's football hooligans tend to do – and Justinian restricted their privileges. Then, during the ides of January, someone from the crowd started cursing Justinian. The emperor responded harshly and made the crowd furious, forcing him to retreat to the palace. When the Hippodrome was open for new games three days later, thirty thousand people started screaming *"Níka!"* ("Conquer!"). Justinian had to flee again, and the masses went out to the streets, broke into prisons, and then the convicts joined them too.

The imperial police were unable to deal with the situation. The aristocrats were eager to see the emperor overthrown, and they gave the rioters the weapons. The city was in flames. The emperor's advisers advised him to escape while he still could, but the empress raised her voice and disagreed, stating that an emperor cannot allow himself to become a fugitive.[xvii] Then the solution emerged. Belisarius had just returned from Persia and was still not sent to Africa. He was able to take care of Constantinople. The mighty general took his men and went to the streets. The great majority of rioters were gathered at the Hippodrome, where the army entered and killed them all. Thirty thousand men were dead, and the city went deadly quiet.

In the aftermath, nineteen senators who supported the rioters were killed and thrown into the sea. No one ever dared again to cause Justinian any trouble.

The Byzantine Golden Age

The disaster at the Hippodrome was also an opportunity. Justinian began a large building program which transformed the city into a truly magnificent metropolis. An extravagant new Senate building replaced the burned one. A huge subterranean cistern was built to provide fresh water to the people as well as the numerous fountains. The most important building that had been demolished in the rebellion was the Hagia Sophia. The church was built by Constantius II and rebuilt by Theodosius II. Justinian abandoned the old project and made perhaps the most impressive cathedral ever built.

Hagia Sophia today (adapted into a mosque), Istanbul, Turkey[xviii]

Belisarius Retakes the Provinces

After the domestic peace was reestablished and the construction works almost complete, Justinian focused on his dreams of imperial expansion. He sent Belisarius to Africa, but he did not spend too much on the campaign. Belisarius had only eighteen thousand men and essential supplies. Nevertheless, the able general managed to defeat the Vandals in Africa, mostly thanks to remarkable discipline. Carthage was reconquered and once again Roman.

Justinian granted his favorite general a triumph and immediately sent him to Sicily. At the same time, another general was sent to northern Italy. Belisarius triumphed, but the other general who was to support him from the north unfortunately failed, was killed, forcing the headless army to withdraw. But the next year, Belisarius entered Rome. His achievement was incredible, but he only had five thousand men. After a few dramatic actions, he wrote to Justinian asking for more men. However, his plea for reinforcements was interpreted as an intention of Belisarius to take the throne. He was only sent a few thousand men and still, in only five years he subdued thousands and returned Africa and Italy to the empire. He might have been able to retake Spain and most of Western Europe if it wasn't for the empress who believed that the general was too powerful to be trusted.

The Hard Times: the Plague

When Justinian finally sent reinforcements to Belisarius, it consisted of seven thousand men led by an elderly general named Narsus. Narsus was an influential figure himself, and he seriously undermined Belisarius' authority. The already small army split in half. The part of army led by Belisarius entered Milan, but was required to return to the Eastern Empire and fight the Persians. When this campaign ended, there was no need for further war. All the enemies, including the Vandals and the Goths, were crippled. The Byzantine Empire was mightier than ever, but the period of prosperity was short-lived. A new and much different enemy emerged. Rats carrying fleas infected with plague came to Egypt, the major source of imperial grain, and the disease spread throughout the empire. In Constantinople, ten thousand people a day died for a period of four months. When the plague finally ended, the populace had to face famine and poverty.

When the disease raged throughout the empire, Belisarius was safe on the Persian frontier. But Justinian was stricken by the disease. Theodora was afraid that Belisarius would take the throne if Justinian died, and she utilized her power to banish the general in disgrace, accusing him of treason.

The Persians took the opportunity to attack the weakened empire, but they only managed to end up infected. At the same time, the Goths seized Italy once again, and there was no Belisarius to resist them. Meanwhile, Justinian recovered, called for Belisarius, and sent him to Italy once again, followed by only four thousand men, only to discover that the people in Italy do not want to pay taxes to the impoverished empire. Justinian was out of options.

Shortly after, Theodora died. Justinian called Belisarius back, gave him a luxurious palace, and built a statue in his honor. Then he sent the general Narses – who had previously undermined Belisarius' authority in Italy – with a large army to claim victory in Rome, and another, Liberius, to retake Spain.

However, Justinian's imperial plans had to be suspended. The plague returned, followed by an earthquake. The impoverished state and drastically reduced number of men that were able to serve the army were not sufficient to protect the frontiers. Soon the Huns started entering the Byzantine territory, and only Constantinople was safe thanks to its walls and natural defenses. Luckily, Justinian still had Belisarius, who was equally brilliant as he had been previously. The general led a few hundred guards and veterans, crushed the Huns, and expelled them from the territory. But he also inspired jealousy in his emperor, who suddenly fired Belisarius and took command of the army.

Eventually, Justinian managed to bring Rome back and maintain peace until the end of his life and reign. He was the last Roman Emperor to speak Latin as his first language, and one of the greatest visionaries the empire ever had.[xix]

Chapter 5 – Heraclius

The emperors who, successively, came after Justinian – Justin II, Tiberius II Constantine, Maurice, and Phocas – are hardly worth mentioning. The West was lost again – this time forever – and the East lived its life more or less the same way it did before. Businesses were thriving, merchants were traveling the roads built by previous emperors, and students were learning at the universities. Even the lower classes were somewhat relaxed during the time of peace, which unfortunately did not last.

In the sixth century, wars and disasters made life difficult for everyone, especially for the poor. Small farms were swallowed by big landowners with either consent of or indifference from the emperor. Taxes were diligently collected from the poor, while the aristocrats enjoyed unjust tax exemptions. The emperors led meaningless wars, their armies destroying everything on the way – just like the barbarian armies had before. The people loathed the distant emperors from Constantinople and did not see them as their true leaders. Uprisings became common. By the end of the sixth century, the empire was on the edge of collapse. A mentally ill usurper called Phocas took the throne. Armies were disorganized. Goods were stolen. Slavene tribes invaded the Balkans. Mess and poverty were everywhere. But there was one part of the empire that was still thriving: North Africa. The Senate in Constantinople saw that as a chance and secretly wrote to the North African emperor, asking him to take control over the Byzantine army and save the empire from misery.

The governor of Carthage was an elderly man and was not interested in great actions, but his son, Heraclius, was. He took a fleet and went to Constantinople. He had no trouble dealing with Phocas; the mob had already lynched him as soon as they noticed the new emperor approaching in 610. But the empire had other, more serious problems: the Persians had invaded Armenia and Mesopotamia, much of the central Byzantine territory, and parts of Egypt. Even the plague had returned. It could hardly be worse. Then refugees from the east brought news that the Persians had seized Jerusalem and killed all its men. In 619, the Persians sacked Egypt. There was no free bread for the people of Byzantium anymore. The empire had no money to pay the soldiers, and Heraclius turned to the church. The patriarch Sergius gave him the entire treasures from the church, including gold and silver plates.

The War against the Persians

Heraclius did not rush to fight the Persians. Hidden behind the walls of Constantinople, he systematically reorganized the army. It took him ten years, but the result was remarkable. The army that left the safety of the city in 622 was confident and inspired by great leadership. They launched a surprise attack from the sea and crushed the Persians with unbelievable ease. Then the Byzantines went to the Persians' sacred place in present-day Azerbaijan and burned the temple of Zoroaster, avenging Jerusalem. But the position of this brave army was dangerous. They were outnumbered and could easily be surrounded from all sides, and there was no one left to protect Constantinople.

Heraclius made the decision to split the army into three parts – one was to defend the capital, and the second two were to invade different parts of the Persian Empire. The fraction led by Heraclius' brother, Theodore, won a great victory; Heraclius won another, entered

Ctesiphon, and returned the True Cross, which the Persians had stolen from Jerusalem. The years when Persia caused terror were over once and for all. The Byzantine Empire finally had a glorious emperor it deserved.

Cultural Changes

By the time of Heraclius, very few people knew Latin. Greek was now the official language of the empire. Even the emperors – who used to be hailed as Imperator Caesar and Augustus – now held the title Basileus.

In 630, Heraclius went to Jerusalem to return the True Cross to where it belonged. He was yet to discover that the church was not unique, and that it was a true weakness that any future invader would exploit.

The Muslim Attack

In 622, when Heraclius was fighting Persians on the Arabian Peninsula, a man named Muhammad went from Mecca to Medina and began slaughtering the local tribes. He divided the world into two parts – *Dar al-Islam* (the House of Islam) and *Dar al-Harb* (the House of War). His followers believed their duty was to expand the House of Islam through holy jihad. In five years, the Muslim armies were ready to start their mission. The surrounding empires were weaker than ever. The Persians asked the Byzantines and the Chinese for help, but the help never came. After Persia, the Muslim army entered the Byzantine province of Syria, destroyed Damascus and, soon after, Jerusalem. By that time, Heraclius was seriously ill and unable to defend the territories. The only thing that he could do in Jerusalem was to take the True Cross with him to Constantinople. For the rest of his life, Heraclius had the feeling that God had abandoned him..

Much of the Middle East went through a deep change. Arabic replaced Greek, and Islam replaced Christianity. Eventually, Damascus and Baghdad, rather than Rome and Constantinople, had become the center of the world for them. As for the Byzantine Empire, there was no one capable of replacing Heraclius on the throne. The next five rulers were underage and without any real influence. Then the period known as the Twenty Years' Anarchy came. Numerous usurpers fought each other, pushing the empire into further chaos. Most of the East had fallen under the Islamic sword, including the whole of Egypt. Even Constantinople was in jeopardy, but eventually a new competent ruler emerged and consolidated the Byzantine force.

Chapter 6 – The Iconoclasts: Leo III the Isaurian and Constantine V

By the end of the seventh century, the Muslim forces held three of the five great Christian cities – Jerusalem, Alexandria, Antioch, and virtually every important capital in the East.[xx] Constantinople wasn't unconquerable anymore – the Muslims had built a navy powerful enough to defeat the Byzantine's. Terrified, the emperor and the entire government moved from Constantinople to Sicily. The only thing that prevented the Arabs from completely destroying Constantinople was a civil war among their lines – one that still hasn't ended, between the Shiites and the Sunnites.

The next target of the forces of Islam was Afghanistan. The Byzantine administration returned to Constantinople, but the Muslims continued to overwhelm their forces. Syracuse in Sicily was destroyed, and the Arabs soon conquered North Africa. Determined to terminate Constantinople, the Arab caliphate launched yearly attacks on the city, which was now exposed from the sea. The Islamic army invaded the island of Rhodes, located across from Constantinople. Only a miracle could save the Christians. But then, a Syrian refugee from Heliopolis, called Callinicus, invented "Greek fire," an extremely flammable liquid (the exact formula was kept as a state secret and it was never revealed), which was released at the enemy fleet from great distances.

Balls of textile were soaked and launched at the ships, which burnt one after another, and the sea water only made it worse for them. Constantinople was saved.

Unfortunately, the rest of the empire was utterly unprotected, and it quickly fell. In the early eighth century, the Islamic forces took Spain. Soon they felt strong enough to try again and finally invade Constantinople.

Meanwhile, a man from Syria called Konon saw his opportunity and, in the midst of chaos, seized the throne and changed his name to Leo III. Thanks to his experience fighting Arabs and the coldest winter in many years, the Muslim army was overcome and forced to return to Damascus.

The Byzantine Iconoclasm

The Byzantine Empire had endured terrible losses. Two-thirds of the territory and half the population were gone. The once-dominant empire was constrained to Asia Minor, which was now poorer and weaker than ever. The Muslims insisted that Christ was just an ordinary prophet and, for a moment, it looked like God was on their side. Was there something that the Muslims were doing right and the Christians wrong? Why had Christ withdrawn his protective hand? Was there something that had angered God? Everyone pondered over those questions, and the emperor managed to identify a single thing that could cause such destruction.

There was actually a divine commandment that the Muslims thoroughly followed and the Christians did not. The worship of icons more and more resembled the old pagan veneration of idols. As soon as he got the idea, Leo III was sure that the empire was being chastised for the sin of idolatry and determined to do whatever it took to make both the sin and the punishment stop immediately. In 725, in the Hagia Sophia, he gave a sermon that changed history. The Muslims, he stated, conquered wastelands thanks to their strict prohibition of all images. The Byzantines, on the other hand, were guilty of heresy. Then he ordered the magnificent golden icon of Christ that was placed on the main gate to the Great Palace, just above the mosaics celebrating the victories of Justinian and Belisarius, to be destroyed. It was just the beginning.

The taking down the icon of Christ provoked public outrage, and a group of women lynched the officer in charge. Occasional riots couldn't stop the emperor, who enjoyed great authority in the army, thanks to his numerous victories. But the pope in the West, as well Western Europe in its entirety, was annoyed by such actions of the Eastern emperor. Unwilling to give up their artistic heritage and pretty much unaware of the deep reasons behind all this (medieval Western Europe was protected behind the Byzantine shield and blissfully unaware of the danger from Arab expansion), the pope condemned the actions of the emperor who interfered with the church's teachings. Leo ordered the arrest of the pope, and the pope excommunicated everyone who dared to destroy an icon. This led to the most profound alienation between Christians in history to that point.[xxi]

In the East, innumerable images were confiscated and destroyed, and the mosaics that decorated church walls were covered with solid colors. Many images found their way to the West. Monks were leaving the monasteries, taking their icons with them. The emperor, however, was unstoppable. Leo III was winning one battle after another, and in 740 he completely expelled the Muslim forces, proving that his iconoclasm (the destruction of icons) had helped the Byzantines. One nightmare was over, and the next year the victorious emperor died peacefully in his bed.

Constantine V

The situation was far from resolved when Leo's son came to the throne. Many hoped that he would stop the appalling practice of smashing the precious artifacts. However, this emperor was raised with an intolerance for idolatry, and he soon became the most aggressive iconoclast who punished and humiliated the monks and even patriarchs who tried to resist him, confiscated the property of the most powerful monasteries, expelled monks and nuns, and lodged his troops in their lodges.

Constantine V had an impressive theological education and was able to defend his beliefs, but he still needed a legitimization from the official church. So he summoned a great council, let only his supporters express their views, and enforced a clear endorsement of iconoclasm. Icons, relics, and even prayers to the saints were all proclaimed idolatry and forbidden.

Just like his father, Constantine V was an extraordinary military commander and won some significant battles over the Bulgars and the Muslims, and his authority was indisputable. But the iconoclasm was tearing the empire apart and, at the same time, creating a distance between Asia Minor and the larger Christian communities worldwide. Because of his zeal, Constantine V had missed the historical chance to unite Christendom under his rule.

Chapter 7 – The Coldblooded Empress Irene of Athens

By the end of his rule, Constantine's military achievements had been forgotten and he was widely loathed by the populace. The iconoclastic emperor became known as *Copronymos*. He was succeeded by his son, Leo, a moderate iconoclast who tried to lower the tension that his father had created. However, he died too soon, possibly due to the intervention of his wife, Irene. Their son, Constantine VI, was only ten and way too young for the throne. So the empress de facto ruled the empire.

Irene was just an orphan from Athens until she won an empire-wide beauty contest, which Constantine V organized in order to choose a wife for his son.[xxii] Irene was a disastrous choice, and she was to soon become one of the most callous rulers in Byzantine history.

As a devoted opponent of iconoclasm, she carefully got rid of iconoclasts who held important positions, including her husband the emperor and the empire's best soldiers and officers. The imperial army was so weak and unmotivated that, when the Muslims came to invade parts of the empire, the soldiers simply joined them. Irene ended up having to pay for peace.

The End of Iconoclasm

The empress' main goal was to restore icons to veneration. She gathered the patriarchs of Rome, Jerusalem, Antioch, and Alexandria to the Church of the Holy Wisdom in Nicaea. The patriarchs unanimously condemned iconoclasm, but admonished the believers to turn away from worship.

But there was one thing that Irene cared for more than for the theological goals: power. She should have ended the regency period once her son turned sixteen. Constantine was already in his twenties, and she still had not let relinquished her duties. Her son was weak and easy to manipulate, but she did not use the possibility to rule from the shadow. She had to have the main role. So, she issued new coins with her images only. Then she issued a decree announcing that, as the senior emperor (not empress), she would always be superior to Constantine VI. When some generals objected, she executed them and had her son thrown into prison.

Mother and Son

As a result of the empress' outrageous actions, the military was both extremely weak and disloyal to her. The Byzantine Empire had suffered terrible losses against the Bulgars, the Arabs, and the Franks. Then soldiers revolted and masses flooded the streets of Constantinople, demanding Irene to step down. Constantine VI was released from his jail cell and raised to the throne, while his mother was put under house arrest.

Ironically, Constantine was incompetent, unambitious, and certainly not the kind of ruler the people had hoped for. Soon he deserved the tag of a coward and restored his mother to the throne. When a plot against both of them was discovered, Constantine proved himself equally ruthless. Then in 797, when the emperor's baby son died, Irene used the opportunity to give the final blow. Constantine was blinded and killed. But her decline had also begun. Even though she was the sole ruler, her army was useless, and the treasury was empty.

Meanwhile in Rome

Pope Leo III had humble origins, and by the end of the eighth century, the hostility between himself and Roman aristocracy became so intense that, one day, a gang ambushed the pope with the intention to blind him and rip out his tongue. The pontiff miraculously escaped to the king of the Franks. His enemies then charged him with several accusations, but the only one who had the authority to preside over such a trial was the emperor of the Roman Empire. At that moment, the emperor in charge in Constantinople was Irene.

The fact that the emperor was a woman bothered the pope more than her immoral past. He needed a different kind of emperor, and he came up with a cunning plan to take power from the East and give it to his allies, the Franks. Charles the Great, also known as Charlemagne, seemed perfect. Already a glorious figure, he appeared in Rome to testify on the Pope's behalf. Then, during a Christmas Mass, Leo declared Charlemagne the Holy Roman Emperor.

Pope Leo acted as if he had the authority to give and take the true crown of the Roman Empire. It was a bold move, and he needed some kind of proof. So, he made the most infamous forgery of the Middle Ages. He made a document called the "Donation of Constantine," which stated that Emperor Constantine had given Pope Sylvester (who, according to the document, had miraculously cured Constantine of leprosy) the authority over the Western Empire. It took six hundred years for the forgery to be revealed, but at that moment in history, it appeared completely authentic.

The people of Constantinople were shocked by the news that an illiterate barbarian was given the title of Roman Emperor. The next step from the west was the offer for Irene to marry Charlemagne, and she almost accepted. But this was too much for the Eastern elite. They captured and banished the empress and proclaimed the minister of finance as emperor. Irene died next year in exile in Lesbos.

Chapter 8 – Tiny Steps Forward: Theophilus and Michael the Drunkard

The empire had changed a lot by the beginning of the ninth century. The Bulgars, empowered by a great warlord called Krum, killed one Byzantine emperor, overthrew another, and caused great damage to the Byzantine army, populace, and land. New emperors turned to iconoclasm again and started burning works of art, but it didn't help. They lacked the powerful armies of Constantine V and his father had.

The situation improved rather slowly. In the ninth century, the empire was reduced to Asia Minor, Greece, and Thrace, but the situation there was stable. Regardless of who was the current emperor, the government was smaller and more efficient. New gold mines were found, resulting in a full treasury.

The Cultural Renaissance under Theophilus

The greatest improvements emerged in the sphere of education. The public interest in literacy was spreading and numerous private schools were open. In the mid-ninth century, Theophilus opened public scriptoria and started paying teachers throughout the empire. The

University of Constantinople received two new faculties. Once again, the city was the cultural capital of Europe.

Unlike any other emperor in the medieval times, Theophilus was surprisingly approachable. On one occasion, he even participated in the chariot races and amazed the spectators with his skill.

This emperor also had a habit of walking the streets of Constantinople in disguise, and once a week he went to different cities and talked to people, encouraging anyone to seek him out and sharing justice.

Finally, Theophilus started the most ambitious projects since the age of Justinian, renovated public buildings, built new ones, and gave the capital a new, lavish appearance.

New Christians

The Slavene people that settled in the Balkans weren't particularly aggressive and could be won over culturally. The pope realized this first and sent missionaries to convert them. The patriarch Photius then sent two of his men – the monks Cyril and Methodius. Even though the western missionaries came first, they insisted that Latin was the only language to be used in services. The Slavs didn't like the idea, and no further progress was made in that direction. The Byzantine monks took a different path and learned Slavic. The language had no written alphabet, so they provided one. Bulgaria and other Balkan states soon entered the Byzantine cultural orbit to which they still belong. The bonds among the states on the east were fortified in Constantinople, but the hostility between the two Christian seas – the old and new Rome – only grew bigger.

Military Recovery under Michael the Drunkard (and his Uncle)

The ninth-century Byzantine Emperors were mostly militarily incompetent. Michael the Drunkard was not an exception, and his nickname was well earned. However, under his rule, a visionary general (who happened to be Michael's uncle) called Bardas won some important battles against Muslim armies, invaded Egypt, and devastated the armies of the emirs of Mesopotamia and Armenia when they attempted to invade the Byzantine territory.

Bardas was effectively governing the empire until Michael decided to give another man, a former peasant called Basil the Macedonian (who was, in fact, Armenian and had no connections with Macedonia whatsoever) too much power. Bardas knew what was coming, but he could not convince his foolish nephew to be more careful. Basil killed Bardas personally, became Michael's co-emperor, and then had the Drunkard killed too.

Chapter 9 – A New Golden Age: Basil the Macedonian and his Dynasty

Basil's past certainly hadn't been spotless, and the future members of his dynasty (which lasted for nearly two hundred years) were uncomfortable with the way he seized the throne. Moreover, by eastern standards, he was embarrassingly uneducated,[xxiii] but it didn't prevent him from ruling effectively. He was aware of the possibility to recover the empire, which was now smaller and easier to defend.

The emperor invested considerable amounts in rebuilding the Byzantine fleet, aware that the Muslims were not as powerful as they were only a century ago. The navy, led by Admiral Nicetas Oöryphas, quickly demonstrated its worth. In a brief action, the Byzantines got rid of the pirates raiding in the Gulf of Corinth. The time had come for a great offensive. The navy attacked Muslim territories, and by 876, vast territories, including Cyprus, northern Mesopotamia, Dalmatia, and Lombardy.

The next step in returning the glory of the empire involved the construction projects. Basil renovated old churches, adorned them with sumptuous mosaics, and overhauled public monuments. Then he built a church as impressive as Hagia Sophia. Iconoclasm had ended long ago, and the new church was rich with decoration. Basil was so engrossed in completing this church that he sacrificed Syracuse to finish it. He needed the navy to transport marble, and he simply refused to send it to Sicily.

A new cultural renaissance started thanks mostly to the patriarch Photius, who made classical Greek and Roman literature popular after so many years. Intellectual awakening spread throughout Byzantium, and the emperor initiated the translation of Justinian's law codex, originally written in Latin, into Greek. The project was not finalized during Basil's reign due to the unexpected setback. The emperor's eldest and favorite son, Constantine, unexpectedly died and left the father depressed for the rest of his life.

The Drunkard's Son, Leo VI the Wise

The next in line for the throne was his second son, Leo VI, who most probably wasn't Basil's son at all. Basil had married a mistress of Michael the Drunkard, and she was already pregnant with this son, who was now 15. The next couple of years were characterized by the antagonism between the (official) father and son. Leo had been beaten and put into prison, then released with the help of the father of his girlfriend, Zöe. It looks like Zöe's father helped his future son in law get rid of his "father" and take the throne. Basil lost the throne in nearly the same way he had helped himself to it: with lots of spilled blood.

Leo's first action as emperor was to exhume Michael the Drunkard and rebury him in the Church of the Holy Apostles. Now that he had avenged his true father and solved his private matter, he focused on politics. Intelligent and superbly educated, Leo VI was completely prepared for the role of the Byzantine emperor. Literature and architecture flourished, and the translation of Roman law was completed. The period of peace and prosperity that enabled these activities didn't just happen; it was all thanks to Leo. He brilliantly came to an idea to appoint his youngest brother, Stephen, as patriarch. Now the emperor controlled both the state and the church, and the two worked in perfect unison.

Leo the Wise, as everyone started to call him, was a great emperor, except for the fact that he wasn't much of a fighter. He actually never led his army in a battle, and his foreign policy was not as impressive as his domestic endeavors. A new hostility between the Byzantines and the Bulgars emerged when the new khan tried to restore paganism. Luckily, the Khan's own father, who had previously retired to a monastery, disposed of him and put his younger brother, Simeon, on the throne. Simeon was a Christian who spent his youth in Constantinople, but the hostility didn't stop until some non-tactical actions were taken by the emperor. Leo then employed the Magyars from the east to teach the Bulgars a lesson. Simeon, in turn, called for the Pechenegs and got rid of the Magyars. The situation was more stable on other fronts, thanks to the impressive fleet and able generals in the east. But something else was going on in the capital, and it was more interesting (if not more important) than all the battles that were led at the time.

The Love Life of an Emperor: Leo and two Zoes

Basil had not allowed Leo to marry his beloved mistress, Zoe, and he forced him to marry another woman, who was now his empress but only for a short time. The couple had no children, and she died shortly after. The emperor was finally free to marry the love of his life and have children with her, but the first child happened to be a girl, and there was no possibility that Zoe would ever give birth to another because she died in fever soon after the girl was born.

Leo was determined to produce an heir and wanted to marry again, but third marriages were forbidden by the Eastern Church. It took a great deal of patience, diplomacy, and blackmails to persuade the new patriarch to let him marry again, this time to Eudocia. His new empress gave birth to a boy and immediately died. The baby, sadly, also died just a few days later. And there seemed to be no way for Leo to ensure a blessing for a fourth marriage. The patriarch informed him that a fourth marriage would be worse than an extramarital affair, which Leo interpreted quite literally and found himself a beautiful lover, named Zoe Carbonopsina ("of the coal-black eyes"). Ironically, the couple had a son shortly after, whom they named Constantine VII.

The patriarch refused to baptize and legitimize the boy and this marriage, and requested Leo to give up Zoe, which he wasn't willing to do. The emperor then turned to the Western pope, who gave him support. Leo arrested the patriarch Nicholas for treason and replaced him with another one. Finally, he made his son his legitimate heir of the Byzantine empire and, a couple of years later, he died.

All the Regent Rulers of Young Emperor Constantine VII

The six year old Constantine was left with a hostile regent, his wicked uncle Alexander III, who immediately expelled Zoe from the palace. Furthermore, the boy was seriously ill and it was a miracle that he even survived. Alexander allegedly intended to have him castrated to prevent him from ever taking power, but thanks to his dynamic lifestyle, the malicious regent soon died of exhaustion.

The next regent was the patriarch Nicholas, whom Alexander had previously restored to power. He untactfully promised the Bulgarian ruler Simeon that the young emperor would marry his daughter, and ended up almost lynched when the people heard about his scandalous plan.

Previously exiled, Zoe Carbonopsina returned to the palace and started acting as regent for her son. Refusing to keep the promise that the patriarch Nicholas had given to the Bulgars, she entered the war. An issue broke out when a Byzantine admiral named Romanus Lecapenus refused to transport the Pechenegs, whom Zoe hired to invade Bulgaria, and left the Byzantine army at the mercy of the Bulgars, who of course took the opportunity and decimated the abandoned soldiers. Zoe's credibility was irreparably ruined, and she decided to marry Leo Phocas, a patrician and successful commander who won some great battles at the Black Sea coast.

Constantine VII was thirteen at the time, and there was a danger that the empress' new husband would eliminate him, so his supporters reached out to the spotless Admiral Romanus Lecapenus. He agreed to protect the young emperor, became the head of the imperial guard, and had the young Constantine marry his daughter. Subsequently, he took all power and became the senior emperor. However, Romanus I Lecapenus wasn't cruel by nature and would never physically hurt Constantine, but he promoted his sons Christopher, Stephen, and Constantine as his co-emperors and gave them an advantage over Constantine VII. Romanus I victoriously ended the war with Bulgaria and was responsible for the great conquests of John Curcuas in the east.

Suddenly, Romanus' eldest son, Christopher – who was meant for the throne – died. His younger brothers, Stephen and Constantine, were spoiled, corrupt, and cruel, and Romanus started feeling guilty for usurping the throne. In his late age, he revoked his earlier decisions and made Constantine VII his exclusive heir. The outraged sons had their father captured and sent off to a distant monastery. But the people of Constantinople did not want any of them on the throne. The time had finally come for Constantine VII to rule in his own right.

Constantine VII "the Purple-born"

While Constantine was heavily ignored in the palace, the Byzantine populace loved him and felt the injustice made against him. He was, after all, a "purple-born," a true son of Macedon, and the Lecapeni were merely usurpers. When the news broke that Constantine's life was in danger, the angry crowd forced the widely despised Lecapeni brothers to acknowledge him as the senior emperor.

Constantine VII[xxiv]

Constantine was already thirty-nine, and was more decisive than anyone expected. He sent the Lecapeni brothers into exile and then continued the policy that Romanus led remarkably well. The only difference was that he replaced some men at the top of the army, favoring the Phocas family, which was at odds with the Lecapeni. A fantastic general, Nicephorus Phocas, together with his nephew, John Tzimisces, emerged victorious against the emir of Syria, conquered cities on the river Euphrates and came near Antioch. Nicephorus soon became known as the "Pale Death of the Saracens," and Muslim forces would abandon the field when they got word that he was on the way.

The Byzantine empire was powerful again. Even though the army was busy on the Syrian border, it still had the capacity to crush the Magyars, who optimistically tried to invade Thrace. But the cultural power of Constantinople grew even bigger. The members of European royal elites were often the guests of Constantine VII, who never ceased to impress them. The eloquent and charismatic emperor left such a powerful impression on the Russian regent princess, Olga, that she promptly decided to convert herself – and subsequently her people – to Christianity.

Constantine died of fever, and the power passed to his son, Romanus II.

Romanus II and Theophano

Unlike his father, Romanus II was born and raised entitled. He never lacked anything and his father abided all his wishes. The problem was that young Romanus wanted to marry Theophano – a woman of modest origin and, as we'll see, not so modest ambition. The marriage was utterly inappropriate, but Constantine did not want to spoil his son's happiness, and the couple happily married and bore a son, whom they named Basil II.

Romanus II found administration rather boring and spent his days hunting. Although he was under the huge influence of his wife, the people who effectively led the empire were two men. One of them was the chamberlain Joseph Bringas, a eunuch who managed to further improve the University of Constantinople, the arts, and the economy of the empire. The second man was Nicephorus Phocas, who continued to win battle after battle and expelled the Arab pirates from Crete. His brother, Leo Phocas, and nephew, John Tzimisces, conquered Syria and Mesopotamia, crushing fifty-five fortresses on the way, and entered Aleppo.[xxv] When they returned, they heard that Romanus II (twenty-two at the time) was dead. According to rumors, he was poisoned by his wife, Theophano. The truth was that he got badly injured while hunting, but this remained a secret because hunting was forbidden during the fast of Lent. The situation was tense, and it was going to be worse.

Chapter 10 – The Change in the House of Macedon: Nicephorus Phocas and His Nephew

No matter how ambitious the empress Teophano was, and no matter how little affection she felt for her husband, she probably never really thought of killing him. Now that he was gone, her position was desperate. Her son, Basil, was still a small child, which made both of them extremely vulnerable. A strong figure was needed to protect the underage emperor, and her mother called for Nicephorus Phocas, the most brilliant Byzantine war commander since Belisarius. The greatest opponent of this idea was the chamberlain Joseph Bringas, who promptly used the influence he still had and released a decree banning the general from the city. However, the closed gates of the city couldn't prevent Nicephorus from entering. He was wildly popular, and crowds soon required that Nicephorus be allowed to enter Constantinople.

When other schemes failed, Joseph wrote to John Tzimisces, the nephew of Nicephorus, and offered him the imperial crown. Tzimisces, however, showed the letter to his uncle, who was proclaimed emperor by his soldiers the following day. The chamberlain continued with desperate measures, jailed all the members of the Phocas family, and eliminated all boats, ferries, and other vessels that could transport anyone into Constantinople. But it was a matter of time when the crowds would erupt, and it soon happened. The Chamberlain lost control over the city, Nicephorus entered, and the patriarchs instantly crowned him.

The Emperor Nicephorus and Theophano

A natural-born leader with vast military experience and numerous victories, Nicephorus was more than qualified to rule Byzantium. But he was so much different from the cultivated men that until very recently sat on the imperial throne. Nicephorus was rude, used to giving orders, short-tempered, and prone to insulting anyone who annoyed him.

The empress-dowager Theophano welcomed him warmly as the protector of her child. He was over fifty, and she was twenty-two. He was an handsome soldier, and she was lovely. Within a month, he proposed her to marry him, which she gladly accepted. But life kept moving on, and soon he was on a campaign again.

Imperial Expansion under Nicephorus

Nicephorus' nephew, John Tzimisces, was already in Syria when the emperor joined him. Together they conquered Aleppo and Cilicia and reduced what used to be a mighty emirate into a vassal state.

The emperor was so good at fighting the Muslims in the east, but his tactlessness proved disastrous in the west. On one occasion, the representatives of the German Emperor Otto I made a mistake and addressed Nicephorus as king of the Greeks. He got so mad that he threw them into a dungeon, which almost resulted in a war against the two empires. The even worse incident occurred when a Bulgarian ambassador came requesting their regular small tribute (which was, in fact, a fixed amount used to cover the cost of a Byzantine princess at the Bulgarian court, which enabled her to live in a way appropriate for her status). Nicephorus became furious and disbelievingly asked if they thought he was a slave. Then he told them he would come in person to pay the tribute they deserved.

Nicephorus paid the Russians to attack Bulgaria for him, and they did so easily. But then the Russians, led by Prince Svyatoslav, simply replaced the Bulgarians, and they were much more aggressive than the former neighbors of Byzantium.

In the next couple of years, he would return to the eastern frontiers to reconquer Armenia and Antioch, but he had some unsolved domestic issues that prevented him from proceeding and retaking Jerusalem.

The Holy Mountain

Nicephorus believed that soldiers who died resisting the forces of Islam should be respected as martyrs. The patriarch firmly refused such a possibility and rejected the notion of "holy warriors" (in the west, as we'll see, such an idea was accepted and that's exactly how the Crusades had begun).

However, this wasn't the only thing that annoyed the emperor. He was constantly marching through Byzantine lands and was fully aware of the prevailing materialism. The church possessed boundless land. Monastic houses were lavish, filled with gold and invaluable frescoes, and bounded by fruitful vineyards. At the same time, the church did not pay any taxes. All this seemed unfair to the emperor Nicephorus Phocas, who decided to put an end to it by issuing several decrees which forbade donating land to the corrupt church.

The emperor thought that monks should live in simple monasteries away from the urban noise. To demonstrate his idea, Nicephoros sent his close friend, the monk Athanasius, to Greece to establish a monastery on the hills of Mount Athos. Then he made the new monastic community (which still exists today and wears the Byzantine flag) autonomous of the patriarch, responsible directly to the throne.

Decline and Death

Despite all his triumphs, the emperor became unpopular in Constantinople. The church was no longer his ally, and everyone else was enraged by ever-increasing taxes. Moreover, there was a rumor that his brother was trying to kill the young princes, Basil and Constantine, yet Nicephorus took no actions against Leo.

A prophecy announced that Nicephorus would be killed in his palace by the hand of one of his own citizens, so he erected a massive wall separating the Great Palace from the rest of the city. The people loathed him, and he used every opportunity to leave Constantinople and find his peace on the real battlefield.

Meanwhile, Theophano had fallen in love with John Tzimisces, the emperor's nephew. The young general was not in favor of the emperor, and the two lovers arranged the murder. Nicephorus was brutally humiliated and butchered during the night by the assassins hidden in the empress' half of the palace. The next day, John Tzimisces was hailed as the Roman Emperor. Theophano was not that lucky. The patriarch ordered Tzimisces to get rid of her if he wanted to be crowned, and he did not object to him.

The Emperor John I Tzimisces

John Tzimisces was both a glorious war commander and a pleasant, well-educated man, the ideal of a true statesman. His first action as the emperor was to get rid of any resistance in Constantinople and once that had been settled, he went to the Balkans. The situation there was quite a mess, thanks to Nicephorus' diplomatic failures. The Russians were openly stating that they would invade Byzantine territory. So, the new emperor led forty thousand troops, smashed the Russians' defenses, and liberated the king of the Bulgars. One more battle and it was all over. The prince of Kiev left Bulgaria with only handful of men; everyone else was dead.

John annexed Bulgaria and moved on. The Fatimids of Egypt were threatening the Byzantine territory in Syria. They already defeated one smaller imperial army and invaded Antioch, and now the time had come for the empire to strike back, and it was one of the most notable military campaigns in the history of the Byzantine Empire. John I Tzimisces started from the north, conquered Mosul, pursued the Muslims down the coast of the Mediterranean and took all the cities of Syria and Palestine on the way: Baalbek, Beirut, Damascus, Tiberias, Acre, Caesarea, Tripoli. He entered Nazareth, the hometown of Jesus Christ, but just like Nicephorus, he postponed the liberation of Jerusalem.

The Byzantine empire was now more powerful than it had been in centuries. All the enemies were devastated, and the emperor was pleased. But when he tried to investigate the origin of the vast properties in the possession of aristocrats, his chamberlain, Basil Lecapenus, poisoned him. Within a couple of days, the great conqueror was dead.

Chapter 11 – Basil II the Bulgar Slayer

The son of Romanus II and Theophano, Basil II, had been growing up while Nicephorus Phocas and John Tzimisces were in charge of the empire. Now that both of them were dead and he was an adult, he could legitimately take the throne, but there were a few obstacles. The first was the head chamberlain, Basil Lecapenus, who was too powerful and equally unwilling to hand over power. The second problem was the notion that in the lengthy history of the Macedon Dynasty, the most competent rulers were the generals and not those who had grown up in the palace.

A general called Bardas Sclerus claimed he was a better choice for the throne, began a revolt, and was promptly hailed as emperor by the masses. Panicked, Basil Lecapenus sent for the exiled general Bardas Phocas, who also wanted to seize the throne, but was the only one who could fight Sclerus. The two armies fought for three years, Phocas won, and returned to fight the Saracens.

The Rise of the Legitimate Emperor

Near the end of the tenth century, Basil Lecapenus was pleased by the way he managed to get rid of both powerful generals. His position was perfect – he held all the power, keeping the incompetent and unambitious emperor as a mask for his deeds – except that the emperor was neither incompetent nor unambitious. Basil II hit the chamberlain out of the blue and had him arrested for conspiring against the emperor. Lecapenus' lands and his wealth were finally confiscated. Basil II was twenty-five and was fully ready to rule the empire.

However, the first military expedition of the new emperor turned out to be disastrous. He went to fight the Bulgars, who meanwhile consolidated under Tsar Samuel. The Byzantine army was caught in an ambush. The emperor fled the field, but most of his army, as well as his reputation, were destroyed.

Then, both Bardas Sclerus and Bardas Phocas decided to try and seize the throne. They even united against the emperor, but Phocas almost immediately arranged for Sclerus to be arrested, and he continued alone.

Alliance with the Russians

The emperor in Constantinople knew he had a problem. The Bulgars were aggressively invading the Balkan peninsula, and he desperately needed an army, but not one led by Phocas. So he reached out to the Russian Prince Vladimir, gave him his sister as a wife, and received a powerful ally and the Varangian Guard – an army of huge, terrifying soldiers who helped him deal with Bardas Phocas first, and then with the Fatimid army in Tripoli, and finally the Bulgars.

Safe with his Varangian Guard, Basil II decided to deal with the nobility, forcing the aristocrats to return the land they had taken during the last few decades. In addition to that, he issued a decree instructing that if a farmer couldn't pay his taxes, his wealthy neighbor was obliged to pay for him.

The Bulgar Slayer

Basil, the Bulgar Slayer, earned his nickname when, after the final battle against Tsar Samuel, he ordered all the prisoners to be blinded, leaving one eye here and there, so that they should find their way home. Now, for the first time since the Slavic tribes came, the entire Balkan Peninsula was under Byzantine control. The empire doubled in size during his reign, and it grew stronger. Basil II knew how important it was to govern new territories properly. Good governance certainly lessened the tension, but Basil used some new means to reach his goals.

In 1012, the Fatimid caliph ordered the destruction of all churches in his territory. Basil II didn't rush into a battle. He reacted with an economical measure and forbade all trade with the Fatimids. When he had to fight, he gladly did, and he always won. The empire now spread from the Danube to the Euphrates. Basil's sixty-four-year reign was the most successful one in Byzantine history. He died of old age while planning a campaign. Unfortunately, he did not have an heir – the fact that always pushed empires into crisis.

Chapter 12 – Alexius Comnenus

The period that came after the death of Basil II was one of constant decline. Mediocrities came to the throne one after another, the economy weakened, and the army completely relied on mercenaries. Then in 1054, the Christian Church split in half. The Latin Catholic ("universal") Church was maintained by the pope, and the Greek Orthodox ("true") was managed by the patriarch. The divide was profound, and the consequences were yet to be felt.

Another setback emerged in the eleventh century when the aggressive Seljuk Turks began invading the imperial territory. A single event that best illustrates the poor health of the empire took place in 1071. The Byzantine army, led by the emperor Romanus Diogenes, managed to push the Seljuks back across the Euphrates. The aristocrats weren't happy about it. A strong emperor could easily limit their privileges, and they did not want to let that happen. So they betrayed him in the decisive moment, sacrificing the best Byzantine soldiers along with the emperor. It was the most obvious sign of almost unreparable decline.

The fight for power between the ambitious aristocrats lasted for ten years, during which many emerged and fell, causing the prolongation of the civil war. New hope emerged in 1081 when the general Alexius Comnenus was crowned.

A Faulty Start

The Comnenus family had always been at odds with the Macedonian dynasty, and Alexius – who seized the throne by killing his predecessor – seemed like yet another usurper. Immediately after his victory, the mercenaries from the army he had employed started robbing Constantinople. It was the first bad sign. The second was the invasion of the Normans, who were now terribly close to the port in Dalmatia that offers direct access to Via Egnatia and the Byzantine capital.

Alexius' army consisted of the Varangian Guard and various mercenaries. The Varangians fought bravely and efficiently against the Normans, but the Turkish mercenaries betrayed them. The bulk of the Byzantine army was butchered.

Alternative Ways

The next time when Alexius had to encounter the Normans, he chose the way of diplomacy. The German Emperor Henry IV, thankful for the gold he had received from the Byzantine Emperor, agreed to attack the common enemy – the Norman Commander Guiscard. The Germans invaded Italy, and the pope was forced to beg the chief Norman to return immediately. Then Alexius reduced Venetian tariffs. The Norman forces depended on Venetian merchants, and now they were left without supplies.

The Norman threat was diminished, and the Muslim enemy was split and inefficient, but the Seljuk Turks were dangerous, and Alexius did not have a proper army. He needed support, and he came to an idea.

The First Crusade

In 1095, Alexius wrote to Pope Urban, informing him of Turkish conquests – most notably the one of the Holy Land – and asking him to send some support to fellow Christians against the Saracens. The pope then delivered a speech in Clermont, France, declaring that "all those who marched with a pure heart would have their sins absolved."[xxvi] The crowd responded enthusiastically. Knights and peasants of all sorts from Italy, France, and Germany started flooding Constantinople. The Crusade seemed like a march on the Byzantine capital, and not the liberation of Jerusalem, and the people involved responded to the pope, not Alexius. One of the crusading knights was the son of Norman Robert Guiscard, from Normandy.

The first group of crusaders consisted of a monk called Peter the Hermit, and a crowd of random, undisciplined people who set fire in many towns on the way to Constantinople and, mistakenly or not, killed many of the Greek population in Asia Minor, only to get beaten by the Turks. The other groups were more serious, but they presented a much bigger threat to the attractive city of Constantinople than to the Turks. Alexius managed to make some kind of deal with them, but some strange conflicts arose on the ground of Asia Minor.

When the crusaders came to Nicaea, the city garrison selected to submit to the Byzantine commander immediately shut the gates to avoid the sack of the city, which was predominantly Christian.

The First Crusade was surprisingly successful. The Crusaders entered Jerusalem in 1099 and killed nearly everyone they found there. Then, in contrast with the given oath, the knights installed themselves as kings of seized towns, which they should have returned to the Byzantine empire.

Hostility grew, and Alexius had to face the Norman Prince Bohemond, who besieged the city and port his father had taken over twenty years ago. Just as before, Alexius cut off his supplies and, by the end of the year, made him surrender and then leave the east, never to return.

Manuel I Comnenus

The Second Crusade happened during the reign of Manuel Comnenus, the grandson of Alexius. He managed to subdue the crusader kingdoms, make the Seljuk Turks accept vassal status, and annex Serbia and Bosnia.

The Crusaders were shocked with the Byzantine's treaty with the Muslims, and the west looked at the Greeks as heretics who didn't care about the "holy war," completely missing the point that there's no such thing as a holy war in peaceful Orthodox Christianity.

The west was building animosity against the Byzantine empire, but the Eastern emperor felt secure for the moment. It looked like the empire was recovering, but it was merely an illusion that wasn't going to last. After his death, everything started to fall again.

Chapter 13 – The Collapse and Fall of the Eastern Roman Empire

There was no great leader to save Byzantium from collapse. During the reign of the underage Alexius II Comnenos, the Turks simply entered Asia Minor, and there was no one to protect it. At the same time, Serbia declared independence, and the Hungarians seized Bosnia and Dalmatia. Emperor Andronicus the Terrible was corrupt and cruel to his subjects but ineffective in foreign affairs. His successor, Isaac Angelus had no authority to rule whatsoever.

During the time of the reign of Isaac Angelus, the Kurdish sultan Saladin united the Muslim forces and Jerusalem fell again. Another crusade was launched, and Isaac proved utterly incompetent by throwing the German ambassadors in prison before apologizing to them. He made one disastrous decision after another and came to the idea to dismiss the imperial navy and let Venice take care of its sea defenses. This idea inspired his brother Alexius III to throw the emperor into a dungeon along with his son. He himself, however, was not much of a ruler either. He was only interested in helping himself to the money for his extravagant parties.[xxvii]

Then another crusading army approached. The third crusade wasn't successful, and now it was time for the fourth, led by Frederick Barbarossa and Richard the Lionheart. Richard wanted to conquer

Egypt, and he needed Venetian ships to take them over, but the Duke of Venetia refused to help without either an outrageously high reward or help to return the city of Zara, which had been taken by the Hungarians.

The Fatal Crusade

At Zara, there was a young fugitive who joined the Crusade – Alexius IV, the son of Isaac II – who had been smuggled from the prison and had been waiting for the opportunity to seize the throne ever since. He promised the crusaders enormous sums and control over the Byzantine church, if only they would help him to the throne. The warriors of the Fourth Crusade were now directed to Constantinople, and they had been told by the Duke of Venice that the Greeks were heretics.

Alexius III fled the city as soon as he realized what was happening. The crusaders released Isaac from prison and now they were waiting for the promised reward. Then they confiscated all they could find, which was only half of the sum that was discussed. They opened tombs to take reliquaries and tore the ornaments from the churches and the jewels from the coverings of ancient manuscripts. In the end, the crusaders burned numerous buildings throughout the city. The most precious churches and palaces burned. Constantinople had never been conquered before, and now it was devastated.

The Aftermath of Destruction and a Short-Lived Recovery

Pope Innocent was shocked and appalled when he heard what happened. He immediately realized what consequences it would have. He excommunicated everyone who was involved, but the damage could never be fixed. Many of the crusaders didn't care whatsoever. They had split estates among each other, crowned a Latin emperor, and put a prostitute on the patriarchal throne.[xxviii]

Surprisingly, the people in small towns and villages were well off. The newcomers on the throne had no means whatsoever to collect the taxes, and now everything stayed in private hands. Culture and the arts flourished, sponsored by private individuals. But the days of imperial power were gone.

The heirs of Byzantine emperors started emerging throughout the Mediterranean, claiming their right to the throne. The patriarch crowned Theodore Lascaris in Nicaea. Then, the Latin Empire of Constantinople fell into the hands of the Bulgars, who did not object that Theodore Lascaris reconquer as much as he could. But another enemy emerged.

In 1242, a frightening Mongol horde came. The Mongols had already overwhelmed a Turkish army. The Seljuk sultan was forced to become his vassal. But they made no damage to Nicaea, where all important Byzantine officials were located. Through various diplomatic activities, Nicaea undermined the Latin Empire. The Crusaders were able to control only Constantinople. They had no sustainable economy, and the only thing they were capable of doing was searching for more hidden relics.

Michael Palaeologus

In 1259, a new emperor was crowned in Nicaea, a young general named Michael Palaeologus. He immediately started diplomatic activities and sent his junior emperor, Alexius Strategopoulos, to observe how strong Constantinople's fortifications were. With the help of local farmers, Strategopoulos managed to open the gates of the city and the next day, the Byzantine forces returned to their city. The Latins panicked and fled on all sides. Since no one came to kill them, they all managed to leave safely.

Michael Palaeologus had never been to Constantinople before. Now he entered as a victor before being crowned in Hagia Sophia. Soon he started with reparation works and redesigned the flag of the empire.

The army he led was small, yet efficient, and managed to deal with all the traditional enemies, such as the Bulgars and the Turks, but a new enemy emerged. Charles of Anjou was invited by Pope Urban IV to take care of Sicily. Then the exiled Latin emperor of Constantinople, Baldwin II, offered him the Peloponnese if he would help him back to the throne. Michael VIII then wrote to the pope to help him and call Anjou back. In return, he submitted the eastern Byzantine church to the authority of the pope. The patriarch, however, refused to ratify the document. Michael Paleologus later managed to ensure the support of Spanish king and overwhelm Charles of Anjou. He was one of the better emperors Byzantium had during its final stage. The last two centuries were full of incapable emperors. During that time, a new enemy emerged, ready to give the final blow to the once powerful empire.

The Ottomans

The balance of power in the east was rapidly changing, and many Turkish tribes were coming to stay. A group of Turks called Gazi (the "swords of God"; later known as the Ottoman warriors) and their leader, Osman, aimed at capturing Constantinople. They took city after a city in the Byzantine empire and quickly came near the walls of the capital. Meanwhile, the bubonic plague spread throughout the empire. When an earthquake hit Gallipoli a couple of years later. The Turks, believing that God had given them a sign, settled in the city. Soon they surrounded Constantinople but were still unable to break in.

Anticipating a catastrophe, the Byzantine Emperor, John V, sent out appeals for help to all Christian kingdoms and empires, wrote a heartfelt letter to the pope, and even converted to Catholicism.[xxix] However, he was largely ignored, and the help from the west never came. The only support came from the Balkans, where Tsar Lazar gathered a coalition of Serbian nobles and their armies and slowed down the Ottoman advance. However, in 1389, at the battle of

Kosovo, Lazar, as well as most other Serbian leaders, were killed. The Ottoman sultan Murad was also killed by a Serbian knight, Milos Obilic, who acted as if he was going to desert the Serbian army the night before the battle. Milos was brought before the sultan and was quick enough to kill the Ottoman leader before his guards managed to react and hack him apart.

John V was taken aback by the news. There was no surviving force to help Constantinople, and he was ready to sacrifice whatever it took to save the city from destruction. He wrote a letter to the new sultan Bayezid, offering to become his vassal in exchange for the Byzantine capital to remain intact. Now the Turks had officially become the masters of the Eastern Christian empire.

The new Byzantine emperor, John's son, Manuel II, showed more integrity than his father, but his plans were soon broken when Bayezid "the Thunderbolt" demonstrated his power again and took the title Sultan of Rome.

Manuel wasn't willing to give up. Bayezid started a long siege against Constantinople, but during a brief period of the sultan's absence, Manuel II and his wife, the Serbian princess Helena Dragases, went to Venice, and then to many European capitals, asking for support against the Muslims. Unlike his father, Manuel was dignified and impressive, and everyone welcomed him warmly. However, it had no real effect. The western rulers were too busy fighting their own battles and they never showed up in the East for support.

An unlikely force saved Constantinople. The Mongol warlord, Timur the Lame, also known as Tamerlane, came from Uzbekistan aiming to restore the empire of his ancient predecessor, Genghis Khan. His empire was huge by the beginning of the fifteenth century, and now he came to conquer Asia Minor. Bayezid needed to defend his new territory, and so he suspended the actions against Constantinople.

Ottoman forces suffered terrible losses against Timur's army, and Bayezid ended up captured and horribly humiliated. But eventually, the Mongols headed to the Far East, determined to conquer China, leaving the Ottomans behind.

The new Ottoman sultan, Bayezid's son, Süleyman, agreed to become Manuel's vassal, but in doing so, he allowed himself time to consolidate and attack again. Manuel II returned to Constantinople as a savior in 1403, but the triumph didn't last long. Süleyman's brother, Musa, overthrew the sultan and attacked Constantinople. Manuel II then helped their third brother, Mehmed, overthrow Musa. The newest sultan was an educated, cultured man, and was ever since loyal to Manuel.

In 1422, after Mehmed had died, his son, Mustafa, sieged Constantinople. Manuel accepted the position of Turkish vassal, but he managed to prevent the Anatolian warriors from entering the city. Constantinople was safe for a brief time but remained surrounded by Turkish forces.

During the reign of Manuel's son, John VIII, Murad II invaded the city of Thessalonica, announcing that Constantinople would be next. Just like many before him, John asked the pope for help, and promised he would submit to the western church. In 1443, the new army of crusaders, this time led by the Hungarian king Ladislas and the general John Hunyadi, conquered Bulgaria. Murad II offered a ten-year truce, but the crusader army had broken it quickly. They went to the coast of the Black Sea, where the superior Ottoman forces waited and devastated them, killing King Ladislas. John Hunyadi continued to resist for a couple of years, but was overwhelmed by 1448, when John VIII was forced to congratulate Murad II on the triumph. He died shortly after that humiliating day.

The Last Emperor of Constantinople

The youngest and most able son of Manuel II, Constantine XI Dragases was crowned in 1449. During the latest Crusade, he managed to retake Athens and the surrounding areas. But now the

Ottomans reconsolidated, reconquered Athens, and were in at the walls of Constantinople. A new age had begun, and the Turkish conquerors brought several cannons with them. It took five days for the walls to be breached. Afterward, the Ottomans then proceeded to the Balkans, leaving the Byzantine capital behind.

Murad II spent some time fighting Skanderg in Dalmatia, and then died. His successor, Mehmed II, a poet and scholar, claimed he was devoted to peace with Byzantium. Yet he was also a cruel ruler who had his younger brother killed just in case.

In 1453, Mehmed's men were armed with superior, newly-built cannons. When Constantine refused to surrender, they opened fire. After forty-eight days, the wall was still in place. Then the sultan changed the approach and entered into the imperial harbor with seventy ships.

The final attack took place on May 29. The remaining citizens gathered in Hagia Sophia, and the last emperor gave a final speech, reminding his populace that they were the heirs of ancient heroes. During that night, the Turks entered the city. The defenders fought till the very end and managed to resist until the Janissaries – the elite troops made of the children taken from the Christians – came and the Genovese mercenaries who helped Constantine until this very moment started retreating. Constantine had more than one opportunity to escape but refused to leave his people. He died during the terrible carnage that followed.

The people of Constantinople believed in an old legend that an angel would protect Hagia Sophia from the Turks, and many citizens gathered there. But no angel appeared, and they were all slaughtered.

Hagia Sophia was converted to a mosque. All men of noble birth were killed, and children were sold into slavery. Constantinople became the capital of the Ottoman Empire, and the sultan took the title of Caesar. The once-unparalleled empire ceased to exist.

Conclusion

After the ages of resistance, the Byzantine empire fell into the Ottoman hands, but at least it prevented the Muslim advance into Europe during the age of their aggressive expansion.[xxx] Now that the Turks managed to conquer the city of Constantine, they lacked the power to proceed to the now much stronger Western Europe. The Ottomans could not break the walls of Vienna, and they started retreating shortly thereafter.

Numerous refugees from Byzantium came into Western Europe and enriched the period of humanism and renaissance by bringing ancient Greek and Roman artifacts and manuscripts, including Plato's Iliad and many others. Not all exiles fled to the West. Many went to Russia, the last free Orthodox state. The peoples and nations that once belonged to the Byzantine cultural orbit are still connected by the Orthodox Church. The immense Byzantine heritage continued to live in various forms throughout the world.

The Timeline of the Byzantine Emperors

The list of all emperors and dynasties of the Byzantine Empire, including less significant ones who haven't been mentioned in this book.

CONSTANTINIAN DYNASTY (324-363)

324—353......Constantine the Great

353—361......Constantius..........*Son of Constantine the Great*

361—363......Julian the Apostate..........*Cousin of Constantius*

NON-DYNASTIC

363—364......Jovian..........Soldier, chosen on the battlefield

364—378......Valens..........Brother of Western Emperor Valentinian

THEODOSIAN DYNASTY (379-457)

379—395......Theodosius I the Great..........*Soldier, chosen by Western Emperor Gratian*

395—408......Arcadius..........*Son of Theodosius*

408—450......Theodosius II..........*Son of Arcadius*

450—457......Marcian..........*Married Theodosius II's sister*

LEONID DYNASTY (457-518)

457—474......Leo I the Thracian..........*Soldier, chosen by Eastern general Aspar*

474......Leo II..........*Grandson of Leo I*

474—475......Zeno..........*Son-in-law of Leo I*

475—476......Basiliscus..........*Usurper, brother-in-law of Leo I*

476—491......Zeno (again)

491—518......Anastasius I..........*Son-in-law of Leo I*

JUSTINIAN DYNASTY (527-602)

518—527......Justin I..........*Commander of the Palace Guard*

527—565......Justinian I the Great..........*Nephew of Justin I*

565—578......Justin II..........*Nephew of Justinian*

578—582......Tiberius II ....*Adopted by Justin II*

582—602......Maurice..........*Son-in-law of Tiberius II*

NON-DYNASTIC

602—610......Phocas..........*Usurper, soldier of Maurice*

HERACLIUS DYNASTY (610-711)

610—641......Heraclius..........*Usurper, general from Carthage*

641......Constantine III..........Son of Heraclius Son of Heraclius Son of Constantine III

641......Heraclonas..........

641—668......Constans II the Bearded..........

668—685......Constantine IV..........*Son of Constans II*

685—695......Justinian II the Slit-Nosed...*Son of Constantine IV*

695—698......*Leontius*..........Usurper, soldier of Justinian II

698—705....*Tiberius III* ....Usurper, Germanic naval officer of Leontius

705—711......Justinian 11 (again)

NON-DYNASTIC

711—713......*Philippicus*..........Usurper, Armenian soldier of Justinian II

713—715......*Anastasius II*..........Usurper, imperial secretary of Philippicus

715—717......*Theodosius III*..........Usurper, tax collector and son (?) of Tiberius III

ISAURIAN DYNASTY (717-802)

717—741......Leo III the Isaurian..........*Usurper, Syrian diplomat of Justinian II*

741—775......Constantine V the Dung-Named..........*Son of Leo III*

775—780......Leo IV the Khazar..........*Son-in-law of Leo III*

780—797......Constantine VI the Blinded..........*Son of Leo IV*

797—802......Irene the Athenian..........*Wife of Leo IV, mother of Constantine VI*

NICEPHORUS DYNASTY (802-813)

802—811......Nicephorus I..........*Usurper, finance minister of Irene*

811......*Stauracius*..........Son of Nicephorus I

811—813 ....Michael I Rangabe..........*Son-in-law of Nicephorus I*

NON-DYNASTIC

813—820......Leo V the Armenian..........*Patrician and general of Michael I*

A̶M̶O̶R̶I̶A̶N̶ D̶Y̶N̶A̶S̶T̶Y̶ (820-867)

820—829......Michael II the Stammerer............*Son-in-law of Constantine VI*

829—842......Theophilus..........*Son of Michael II*

842—855......Theodora..........*Wife of Theophilus*

842—867......Michael III the Drunkard ...*Son of Theophilus*

M̶A̶C̶E̶D̶O̶N̶I̶A̶N̶ D̶Y̶N̶A̶S̶T̶Y̶ (867-1056)

867—886......Basil I the Macedonian..........*Armenian peasant, married Michael III's widow*

886—912......Leo VI the Wise..........*Son of Basil I or Michael III*

912—913......Alexander..........*Son of Basil I*

913—959......Constantine VII the Purple-Born..........*Son of Leo VI*

920—944.....Romanus I Lecapenus..........*General, father-in-law of Constantine VII*

959—963......Romanus II the Purple-Born..........*Son of Constantine VII*

963—969......Nicephorus II Phocas..........*General, married Romanus II's widow*

969—976......John I Tzimisces..........*Usurper, nephew of Nicephorus II*

976—1025......Basil II the Bulgar-Slayer..........*Son of Romanus II*

1025—1028......Constantine VIII..........*Son of Romanus II*

1028—1050......Zoë....Daughter of Constantine VIII

1028—1034......Romanus III Argyrus..........*Zoë's first husband*

1034—1041......Michael IV the Paphlagonian..........*Zoë's second husband*

1041—1042......Michael V the Caulker..........*Zoë's adopted son*

1042......Zoë and Theodora..........*Daughters of Constantine VIII*

1042—1055.......Constantine IX Monomachus..........*Zoë's third husband*

1055—1056........Theodora (again)

NON-DYNASTIC

1056—1057.......Michael VI the Old..........*Chosen by Theodora*

1057—1059......Isaac I Comnenus..........*Usurper, general of Michael VI*

DUCAS DYNASTY (1059-1081)

1059—1067......Constantine X..........*Chosen by Isaac*

1068—1071......Romanus IV Diogenes..........*Married Constantine X's widow*

1071—1078......Michael VII the Quarter-Short..........*Son of Constantine X*

1078—1081......Nicephorus III Botaneiates............*Usurper, general of Michael VII*

COMNENIAN DYNASTY (1081-1185)

1081—1118......Alexius I..........*Usurper, nephew of Isaac I*

1118—1143......John II the Beautiful..........*Son of Alexius I*

1141—1180......Manuel I the Great..........*Son of John II*

1080—1183.......Alexius II..........*Son of Manuel I*

1183—1185......Andronicus the Terrible..........*Usurper, cousin of Manuel I*

Angelus Dynasty (1185-1204)

1185 1195......Isaac II Ángelus..........*Great-grandson of Alexius I*

1195—1203.......Alexius III Ángelus..........*Brother of Isaac II*

1203—1204......Isaac II (again) and son Alexius IV

Non-Dynastic

1204......Alexius V the Bushy-Eyebrowed..........*Usurper, son-in-law of Alexius III*

Palaeologian Dynasty (1259-1453)

1259—1282.......Michael VIII..........*Great-grandson of Alexius III*

1282—1328......Andronicus II..........*Son of Michael VIII*

1328—1341.......Andronicus III..........*Grandson of Andronicus II*

1341—1391....John V..........*Son of Andronicus III*

1347—1354.......John VI..........*Father-in-law of John V*

1376—1379......Andronicus IV..........*Son of John V*

1390......John VII..........*Son of Andronicus IV*

1391—1425......Manuel II..........*Son of John V*

1425—1448......John VIII..........*Son of Manuel II*

1448—1453......Constantine XI Dragases............*Son of Manuel II*

Read more Captivating History Books about Ancient History

Click here to check out this book!

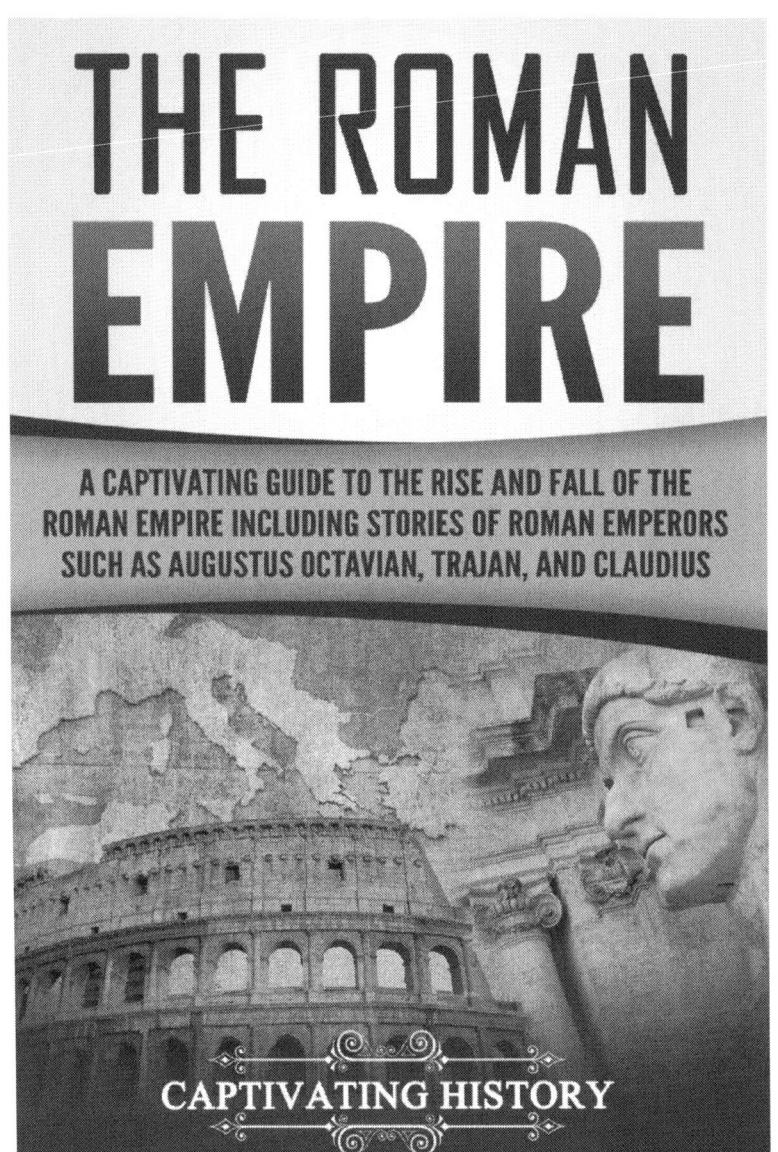

Check out this book!

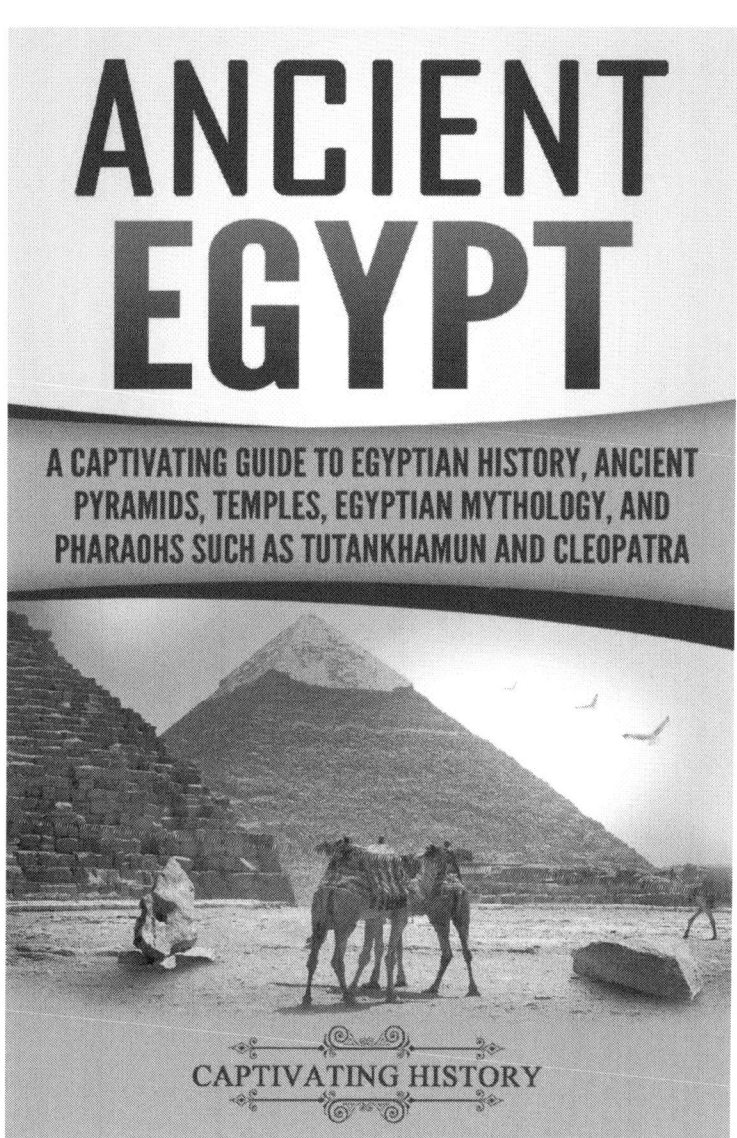

Check out this book!

References

[i] Lars Brownworth, *Lost to the West: The Forgotten Byzantine Empire That Rescued Western Civilization*, Crown Publishing, New York, 2009.
[ii] Brownworth, as above; Edward Gibbon, *The History Of The Decline And Fall Of The Roman Empire*, Vol. Five, Project Gutenberg edition: http://www.gutenberg.org/files/735/735-h/735-h.htm
[iii] Brownworth, as above
[iv] Learn more about Augustus and the Principate in Book 2 of *Ancient Rome* - "The Roman Empire"
[v] Timothy E. Gregory, *A History of Byzantium*. Malden, MA: Blackwell Publishing, 2005.
[vi] Image courtesy of Katie Chao/MOMA/Wikimedia Commons (CC)
[vii] Brownworth, as above
[viii] Image courtesy of Jorge Láscar/Flickr (CC) https://www.flickr.com/photos/8721758@N06/10350972756
[ix] Brownworth, as above
[x] Gregory, as above
[xi] Julian, as cited by Brownworth (see above)
[xii] Image courtesy of Classical Numismatic Group/Wikipedia Commons
[xiii] As cited on https://en.wikipedia.org/wiki/List_of_oracular_statements_from_Delphi ; **Five** different translations available here: http://laudatortemporisacti.blogspot.com/2012/12/the-last-oracle.html
[xiv] Gibbon, as above
[xv] Image courtesy of Petar Milosevic/Wikipedia Commons
[xvi] Gregory, as above
[xvii] "I do not care whether or not it is proper for a woman to give brave counsel to frightened men; but in moments of extreme danger, conscience is the only guide. Every man who is born into the light of day must sooner or later die; and how can an Emperor ever allow himself to become a fugitive? If you, my Lord, wish to save your skin, you will have no difficulty in doing so. We are rich, there is the sea, there too are our ships. But consider first whether, when you reach safety, you

will not regret that you did not choose death in preference. As for me, I stand by the ancient saying: royalty makes the best shroud."—Empress Theodora (recorded by Procopius, as cited in Brownsworth)

[xviii] Image courtesy of Arild Vågen (Wikipedia Commons)

[xix] Brownworth, as above

[xx] The five Great Christian Seas or the Five Patriarchates were Rome, Constantinople, Jerusalem, Antioch, and Jerusalem, which made the Pentarchy of Christianity.

[xxi] Gregory, as above

[xxii] Brownworth, as above

[xxiii] Gregory, as above

[xxiv] Author unknown/public domain

[xxv] Brownworth, as above

[xxvi] As cited by Brownworth

[xxvii] Gibbon, as above

[xxviii] Norwich, John Julius. Byzantium: The Decline and Fall. New York: Alfred A. Knopf, 2003.

[xxix] Norwich, as above

[xxx] Gibbon, as above

Free Bonus from Captivating History (Available for a Limited time)

Hi History Lovers!

Now you have a chance to join our exclusive history list so you can get your first history ebook for free as well as discounts and a potential to get more history books for free! Simply visit the link below to join.

Captivatinghistory.com/ebook

Also, make sure to follow us on:

Twitter: @Captivhistory

Facebook: Captivating History:@captivatinghistory

Printed in Great Britain
by Amazon